DOG CRAFTS

DOG CRAFTS

More Than 50 Grrreat Projects

Bobbe Needham

A Sterling/Lark Book
Sterling Publishing Co., Inc.   New York

Art Director: Dana Irwin
Production: Elaine Thompson, Dana Irwin
Photography: Evan Bracken
Research: Laura Dover
Computer-Generated Illustrations: Bobby Gold

Library of Congress Cataloging-in-Publication Data
Needham, Bobbe.
    Dog crafts : more than 50 grrreat projects / Bobbe Needham.
      p. cm.
    "A Sterling/Lark book."
    Includes index.
    ISBN 0-8069-9565-3
    1. Dogs--Equipment and supplies. 2. Handicraft. 3. Dogs in art.
4. Gifts. I. Title.
SF427.15.N44 1997
745.5--dc20   96-36803
                                      CIP

A Sterling/Lark Book

10 9 8 7 6 5 4 3

Published by Sterling Publishing Co., Inc.
387 Park Avenue South, New York, NY 10016

Created and produced by Altamont Press, Inc.
50 College Street, Asheville, NC 28801

© 1997, Altamont Press

Distributed in Canada by Sterling Publishing,
  c/o Canadian Manda Group, One Atlantic Avenue,
  Suite 105, Toronto, Ontario M6K 3E7

Distributed in Great Britain and Europe by Cassell PLC,
  Wellington House, 125 Strand, London WC2R OBB, England

Distributed in Australia by Capricorn Link (Australia) Pty Ltd.
  P.O. Box 6651, Baulkham Hills, Business Centre, NSW 2153, Australia

Printed in Hong Kong

ISBN 0-8069-9565-3

CONTENTS

Going to the Dogs

Bobbe Needham, her little sister Nancy, and their dog, Susie.

Dana and Amy Irwin with their family dog, Butch.

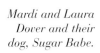

Mardi and Laura Dover and their dog, Sugar Babe.

I'm a dog person. My mother used to claim that dog people could never be content with cats, and that cat people—well, there was always something questionable about them. Mainly the question was, Why didn't they have a dog?

Now that I live with cats, I can confess that as dog people, my family always felt superior to cat people. Dog people, we thought, had more depth, more substance. Somehow they seemed more responsible than cat people, who struck us as frivolous, unserious, afraid to commit to real animals.

I still feel a bond with dog people. Everyone involved with this book has a dog, or misses their dog, or just loves dogs. And everyone who heard about the book and has a dog wanted their dog in the book. And every one of those dogs is the most loving, the best humored, the most special dog in the world. I believe them. I've always felt that way about my dogs. Otherwise, what would be the point?

So this book, and these projects, are celebrations of dogs. It's not very serious. But I think it takes dogs about as seriously, probably, as they can stand.

I've assumed that if you dote on dogs, you might not have had much spare time for perfecting Olympic-level sewing, woodworking, sculpting, or needle-working skills.

So nearly all the projects were designed to be made by beginners. If you can use a sewing machine and thread a needle, you can do all the sewing projects—and most of them take advantage of quick-and-easy nonsewing sewing aids.

You'll find this quilt on page 80.

If you've always wanted to try quilting but felt overwhelmed at the prospect of actually doing it, I urge you to try the Canny Canine Quilt. It's a manageable size, you do it on a sewing machine, and the result is spectacular.

You'll find this bed on page 86.

While some of the wood projects may look intimidating, they're all do-able by beginning woodworkers. The one that may call for the most creative approach (and for that reason one of the most satisfying to build) is the Let-Sleeping-Dogs-Lie Bed—since it's made from an old chair, you may find yourself adjusting the directions.

The knitting and crocheting projects call for only the most basic skills (and the Ecologically Correct Canine Fashion Sweaters require no knitting at all)—in fact, they're ideal learn-to-knit or learn-to-crochet projects for first-timers.

PHOTO BY: LEVERT TUNCER

You'll find this sweater on page 38.

One of the payoffs for making any of these projects is that, far from turning up its nose at them, your dog will be struck speechless (with amazement and gratitude).

7

It's a Dog's Life

Gourmet Snacks to

These nutritious, natural, delicious-smelling, dog-tested, bet-you-can't-eat-just-one snacks are to die for—sorry, to roll over and play dead for.

Before you begin: Though not essential for these snack recipes, bonemeal and lecithin are good for dogs' bones, teeth, and coat. You'll find bonemeal and nutritional yeast at health-food stores.

Sunflower Seed Snowmen

INGREDIENTS

2 cups whole-wheat flour

1/2 cup soy flour

1/4 cup corn meal

1/2 cup raw sunflower
  seeds, hulled

1 tablespoon nutritional
  yeast

1 teaspoon salt

2 tablespoons canola oil

2/3 cup skimmed milk or
  water

1/4 cup honey

1

Combine flours, corn meal,
sunflower seed, yeast, and
salt.

2

Add oil and combine well.

3

Add honey and milk
or water and combine
thoroughly.

4

Let dough rest for half an
hour so it can absorb liquids
and is easier to handle.

5

Lightly flour bread board
or counter and roll out
dough to 1/2" (1.5 cm)
thickness.

Cut out snowmen with a
cookie cutter.

6

Bake at 325° for 45 minutes.

*Yield: Two dozen 3-1/2"
(9 cm) snowmen*

Alfalfa Hearts

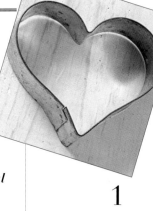

INGREDIENTS

2 cups whole-wheat flour

1/2 cup soy flour

1 teaspoon bonemeal (optional)

2 tablespoons nutritional yeast

1 tablespoon lethicin (optional)

1/2 teaspoon salt

1/4 teaspoon garlic powder

3 tablespoons dried alfalfa leaves, crumbled

1 cup cooked brown rice

3 tablespoons canola oil

1/2 cup water

1

Combine first eight ingredients. Add rice and oil. Combine well.

2

Add 1/4 cup water. Dough should be very easy to handle, not crumbly.

3

Lightly flour board or counter and roll out dough to 1/4" (1 cm) thickness. Cut with 2-1/2" (6.5 cm) heart-shaped cutter.

4

Bake at 350° for 25 minutes.

Yield: 3 dozen hearts

Multigrain Canine Crackers

INGREDIENTS

3/4 cup whole-wheat flour

1/4 cup rye flour

1/4 cup rolled oats

1/4 cup soy flour

1/4 teaspoon garlic powder

1/2 teaspoon bonemeal (optional)

2 tablespoons nutritional yeast

3 tablespoons canola oil

1/3 cup water

1

Combine dry ingredients in mixing bowl—mix with the paddle attachment in electric mixer or by hand with a wooden spoon.

2

Add oil and combine thoroughly.

3

Add water to form a stiff dough. Don't overmix.

4

Lightly flour board or counter. Roll out dough to 1/4" (1 cm) thickness. Cut with a 2" (5 cm) biscuit cutter. Poke a row of holes in crackers with a fork.

5

Bake at 350° for 20-25 minutes until golden brown. Store in airtight container for up to a week; freeze for longer-lasting freshness.

Yield: Two dozen 2" (5 cm) crackers

Canine Carrot Bears

INGREDIENTS

2 cups whole-wheat flour

1/4 cup soy flour

1 tablespoon dry milk

2 tablespoons wheat bran

1/2 cup oats

1/2 teaspoon salt

1/8 teaspoon cinnamon

*1/2 cup finely chopped
cooked carrots*

2 tablespoons canola oil

2 eggs, beaten

1 tablespoon molasses

1

Combine dry ingredients.

2

Add remaining ingredients
and mix until well combined.

3

On lightly floured board or
counter, roll out dough to
3/8" (1.25 cm) thickness.
Cut into bear shapes with
bear cookie cutter.

4

Bake at 350° for 30 min-
utes. Store in airtight container for several days;
freeze for longer storage.

Yield: 16 3-1/2" (9 cm) bears

"MY NAME IS OPRAH WINFREY. I HAVE
A TALK SHOW. I'M SINGLE. I HAVE EIGHT
DOGS—FIVE GOLDEN RETRIEVERS, TWO
BLACK LABS, AND A MONGREL."
—OPRAH WINFREY,
DESCRIBING HERSELF FOR JURY DUTY

RECIPES
MAYA CONTENTO

11

Wholesome
Whole-Wheat Biscuits

INGREDIENTS

2-1/2 cups whole-wheat
flour

1/2 cup self-rising flour

1 tablespoon beef or
chicken bouillon powder

3 tablespoons dehydrated
milk (optional)

2 cloves garlic, crushed

1 egg, beaten

1 tablespoon molasses or
honey

3 tablespoons canola oil

1/4 cup water plus
2 tablespoons

1

Measure dry ingredients into
bowl. Blend with all other
ingredients and chill for one
hour.

2

On a floured surface, roll
dough to 1/8-inch (.5 cm)
thickness and cut with cookie
cutters or into strips 1 by 3
inches (3 by 8 cm).

3

Bake at 300° on cookie
sheets for 30 minutes. Brush
with melted butter if
desired. Cool and serve.

All Natural

**Herbal
Treats**

for your dog

RECIPE
DEBBIE MIDKIFF

"SOMETIMES, WHEN
I THINK ABOUT IT,
IT SEEMS THAT DOGS HAVE A BAD DEAL.
WE TEACH THEM TO SIT AND STAY
AND ROLL OVER. THEY TEACH US DIGNITY
AND HEROISM AND THE UNFETTERED JOY
IN BEING YOURSELF.
HAVE YOU EVER SEEN A GOLDEN
RETRIEVER MOPE AROUND WISHING
SHE WAS A SPITZ?"
—ARTHUR YORINKS,
"THE EYES HAVE IT"

It's a Dog-Eat-Doggie-Donuts World

In this era of canine greeting cards ("Your doghouse or mine?"), doggie boutiques, pet therapy, dog horoscopes, and tranquilizers for compulsive tail chasers, a pet bakery seems almost passé. Still...catering a birthday party for twenty-two dogs? "The birthday dog was fifteen," said Anthony Mascolino, co-owner with his wife, Mary Lou, of Pet's Pride in Hendersonville, North Carolina. "We supplied cookies in an edible dish, a birthday cake with white frosting, party bags—well, doggie bags—with snacks like Oatmeal Man—"

Oatmeal Man? One of their best sellers, along with bulldog burgers, pit-bull brownies, beagle bagels, Italian greyhound garlic bread, and, of course—the Mascolinos are Italian American—doggie pizza.

Pet's Pride got started when the Mascolinos decided to cater to one of their own dogs, a finicky eater. The result was first a mail-order business, finally a retail store. "We guarantee our snacks are healthy," Anthony Mascolino said. "In fact, people can eat all our food."

Two bulldog burgers with everything, to go.

The ideal place to store this book's Sunflower Seed Snowmen, Alfalfa Hearts, Wholesome Whole-Wheat Biscuits, and other taste treats you make for your favorite four-legged friends.

MATERIALS AND TOOLS

Large metal canisters

Fast-drying spray enamel in desired base colors (in hardware stores)

Multipurpose water-based high-gloss enamels for ceramics, metals, etc., 1 oz. bottles, in desired colors (in craft stores)

#3 soft-bristle brush for water-based paint

Pencil

1

Wash canisters with soapy water to remove tape, grease, etc. Dry thoroughly, then in a well-ventilated area or outdoors, spray paint your chosen base color, following directions on the spray can.

2

Lightly draw your designs on the canisters. Paint one color of the design. Wait at least thirty minutes between colors. Allow your finished paint job to dry for an hour before you use the canister.

DESIGN
PAMELLA WILSON

"I THINK WE ARE DRAWN TO DOGS BECAUSE THEY ARE THE UNINHIBITED CREATURES WE MIGHT BE IF WE WEREN'T CERTAIN WE KNEW BETTER."
—GEORGE BIRD EVANS, "TROUBLE WITH BIRD DOGS"

TAIL-WAGGER TIP

Dogs whose owners smoke are 50 percent more likely to develop lung cancer than dogs whose owners have smoke-free homes... and dogs with short or medium-length noses are at greater risk.

Paws-That-Refreshes Placemats

Here are everyday and special-day mats (or luncheon and late-night, or breakfast and buffet)—but your dog may deserve a fancy mat at every meal. Simple to make, wipe-clean, and lovely in a set for a trousseau or puppy shower.

MATERIALS AND TOOLS

1/2 yd. (46 cm) of iron-on vinyl

1/3 yd. (31 cm) of fabric—or 12" by 16" (31 by 41 cm) per mat

Fabric scraps

Fusible web

Pencil

Sewing machine (optional)

Iron

Scissors

"WE HAD CALLED THE DOG STRANGER OUT OF THE FAINT HOPE THAT HE WAS JUST PASSING THROUGH [BUT] HE STAYED ON FOR NEARLY A SCORE OF YEARS, ALL THE WHILE BITING THE HANDS THAT FED HIM AND MAKING SNIDE REMARKS ABOUT MY GRANDMOTHER'S COOKING."
—PATRICK F. MCMANUS, "A DOG FOR ALL SEASONS"

1

Cut mat(s) to size. For the pattern, adapt project designs or draw your own. Lay fusible web, paper side up, on your designs and trace.

2

Cut out designs and place web side down on fabric scraps, as desired. Bond to fabric with hot iron (about five seconds). Cut out fabric designs, peel off paper backing, and arrange on mat.

3

Apply vinyl per package instructions; trim edges as needed and zig-zag stitch, if you wish, to prevent raveling.

DESIGN
NANCY ASMUS

15

Fine Dining Dish

Treat your gourmand to an elegant canine dining experience every day, al fresco or in the kitchen. If you've never used a miter box, which cuts angles of picture frames and other moldings so they'll fit squarely, this project is the perfect place to start—easy to understand, easy to do.

MATERIALS

2 bowls about 6" (15 cm) in diameter

1/2" (1.5 cm) plywood, 10" by 17" (26 by 44 cm)

8' (2.48 m) wood molding (wider than depth of bowls)

1" (3 cm) finish nails

Wood glue

Sandpaper (fine)

Paint and stain as desired

TOOLS

Compass

Jigsaw

Drill with 1/4" (1 cm) bit

Hammer

Miter box and saw

DESIGN
MARK STROM

16

1

Center the bowls, upside-down, on the plywood and draw a light circle around them. With the compass, draw another circle 1/2" (1.5 cm) smaller inside each one. Drill a starter hole, then cut out the smaller circles with the jigsaw.

2

Set the miter-box at 45° and cut the molding: two pieces 17" (44 cm) at inside of angles, and two pieces 10" (26 cm) at inside of angles.

3

Glue the ends of the molding together to make a rectangle that will frame your plywood. Secure with two finish nails at each join.

4

Sand and finish all surfaces. (Mark Strom painted the molding with black lacquer and used a maple urethane stain on the plywood.)

5

Position the plywood 1/2" (1.5 cm) below the top edge of the molding (to catch food), then nail frame and plywood together with finish nails. Insert bowls and serve up your dog's favorite food (al dente?).

"THERE ARE A FEW...HARD-AND-FAST
RULES AT OUR HOUSE...AND THE MAJORITY
OF THEM APPLY TO MEALTIMES. FOR
INSTANCE: NO DOGS ON THE TABLE
DURING DINNER. AT THE TABLE IS
ACCEPTABLE, TO A POINT. NO CLIMBING
UP ON GUESTS, UNLESS THEY ARE
FOOLISH ENOUGH TO ENCOURAGE IT."
—BOB SHACOCHIS.
"THE COMPANY OF CANINES"

TAIL-WAGGER TIP

Feed a litter of newly
weaned puppies from
a muffin pan. Weaker
babies won't have to
compete with stronger
ones for food.

Ear Tidy

A thoughtful gift for your long-eared dog, to keep those ears out of the feeding bowl and save the dog from an undignified breach of etiquette.

MATERIALS AND TOOLS

1/4 yd. (23 cm) fabric

1/3 yd. (31 cm) elastic, 1" (3 cm) wide

Sewing machine

Basic sewing equipment

Iron

DESIGN
KIM TIBBALS

1

For the bow, cut two pieces of fabric, 6" by 14" (15 by 36 cm). For the elastic casing, cut a strip of fabric 4" by 28" (10 by 72 cm). Fold the casing fabric in half lengthwise and stitch along the long side 1/2" (1.5 cm) from the raw edges. Turn right side out and press, with the seam centered on one side. Top stitch along the length of the casing, 1/4" (1 cm) from top and bottom edges.

2

Figure out how long the looped elastic needs to be to hold up the dog's ears without being too tight. Allow a 1/2" (1.5 cm) overlap for joining the ends. Cut elastic to this measurement. Thread the elastic through the fabric tube, then overlap and stitch securely. Tuck in raw edges of fabric tube and slipstitch the ends together.

3

Make points on the short ends of the bow pieces of fabric by marking the center of each end, then measuring 1-1/2" (4 cm) down on each side of each end—mark with straight pins. Cut from each pin to the center mark to make points. With right sides of the bow pieces together, stitch 1/2" (1.5 cm) from raw edge around the bow, leaving a 2" (5 cm) opening along one long edge for turning the bow right side out. Trim the seams to 1/4" (1 cm). Turn right side out.

4

Top stitch almost 1/4" (1 cm) from the edge all around the bow, catching the raw edges of the opening. Tie into a knot. Slip stitch the center of the knot to the covered elastic at its seam.

"FOR A NUMBER OF YEARS PAST I HAVE BEEN AGREEABLY
ENCUMBERED BY A VERY LARGE AND DISSOLUTE
DACHSHUND NAMED FRED.
OF ALL THE DOGS WHOM I HAVE SERVED I'VE NEVER
KNOWN ONE WHO UNDERSTOOD SO MUCH OF
WHAT I SAY OR HELD IT IN SUCH DEEP CONTEMPT."
—E. B. WHITE, "DOG TRAINING"

See-Spot-Eat Bowls

A bevy of bowls to fill with canine comestibles, from the healthful snacks and treats you'll find in this book to party canapés and hearty meals.

MATERIALS AND TOOLS

3 flat-bottomed ceramic bowls, with 8" (21 cm) diameters

Multipurpose water-based high-gloss enamels for ceramics or metals, 1 oz. bottles, in desired colors (in craft stores)

Rubbing alcohol

#3 soft-bristle brush for water-based paint

1 foam ear plug (for polka dots)

Pencil

Lettering stencils, 1" and 1/2" (3 and 1.5 cm)

1

Clean bowl surface with rubbing alcohol, then lightly sketch a simple design on the bowl. Paint one color of the design: apply dots with the foam ear plug. Wait thirty minutes between each new color, rinsing your brush well in water between each.

2

Allow your finished design to dry for forty-eight hours. Then put the bowls in a cold oven and set the oven at 200°F. After one hour, turn the oven off but leave the bowls in the oven and allow them to cool slowly.

DESIGN
PAMELLA WILSON

"I ALWAYS THOUGHT MY CANINE FAMILY TENDED TO VIEW ME AS THE FUNNY-LOOKING TWO-LEGGED DOG WHO RUNS THE CAN OPENER."
—ROGER CARAS, "A DOG IS LISTENING"

A sure crowd pleaser, this apron is one of the simplest projects to make, since you start with a readymade apron (which also makes it a great last-minute gift).

MATERIALS AND TOOLS

Apron

Scraps of fabric in your choice of colors and patterns

Fusible web

Matching threads

Basic sewing equipment

Iron

1

Trace patterns and letters on page 117 onto fusible web. Bond patterns to the appropriate fabrics with a dry, hot iron, paper side up.

2

Cut out pieces, peel off paper, and bond to the front of the apron with a hot iron.

3

Appliqué all designs with matching thread for a professional look.

DESIGN
NANCY ASMUS

"HE WAS BORN IN BERCY ON THE OUTSKIRTS OF PARIS AND TRAINED IN FRANCE, AND WHILE HE KNOWS A LITTLE POODLE-ENGLISH, HE RESPONDS QUICKLY ONLY TO COMMANDS IN FRENCH. OTHERWISE HE HAS TO TRANSLATE, AND THAT SLOWS HIM DOWN."
—JOHN STEINBECK, *TRAVELS WITH CHARLIE*

Birthday Party

Every best friend deserves a party occasionally—and if you're not sure of your dog's birth date, how about a glad-you-were-born bash?

Party Hats

MATERIALS AND TOOLS

For each hat:

12" by 12" (31 by 31 cm) each of fabric and low-temp fusible webbing

Trims (rickrack, glass "jewels," drapery trims, fringes, lace, sequins, etc.)

12" (31 cm) elastic, 1/2" (1.5 cm) wide

Craft glue

Iron

Stapler

Scissors

Needle and thread

1

For each hat, cut a paper circle 8" (21 cm) in diameter; cut in half for pattern. Trim to size that best fits your dog (or guest). Trace pattern onto fusible webbing.

2

Fuse the webbing onto the back of hat fabric, following directions on the webbing, and trim around the edges; this semicircle is the hat base.

3

Glue, sew, and staple trim as desired.

4

Make the cone by stapling or sewing the seam. Staple or sew on the elastic to hold the hat on under the chin.

> "PEOPLE CAN BE A FINE SUBSTITUTE FOR OTHER DOGS. BUT I THINK THAT IF THEY HAD TO CHOOSE, DOGS BY AND LARGE WOULD CHOOSE THE COMPANY OF OTHER DOGS."
> —ELIZABETH THOMAS, *THE HIDDEN LIFE OF DOGS*

Placemats

MATERIALS AND TOOLS

For each mat:

12" by 18" (31 by 46 cm) each of main fabric and of medium-weight clear vinyl sheeting (or iron-on vinyl)

8" by 8" (21 by 21 cm) each of dog-motif fabric (or other motifs for appliqué) and of low-temp fusible webbing

Iron

Scissors

1

Cut out dog motifs or other appliqués and trace onto fusible webbing; following webbing instructions, fuse the webbing to the appliqués, then position on the mats as desired and fuse. Press well.

2

Fit vinyl to mat and serge or zigzag around the raw edges; or, for iron-on vinyl, press.

Napkins/Bandanas

Either buy colorful bandanas or cut squares of fabric and serge or overcast the edges. These make handsome take-home favors for canine guests.

Birthday Cake

Mush together three cans of dog food and add enough cracker or bread crumbs so the mixture will hold a cake shape. Coat with crumbs for frosting. Stick dog biscuits or treats along the sides and on top. Freeze to "glue" (optional). Top with real candles or chew sticks.

DESIGN
SUZANNE KOPPI
AND NANCY ASMUS

23

The Year of the Dog

According to the Chinese calendar, the Year of the Dog comes up every twelve years and starts with the second new moon after the winter solstice. The most recent Year of the Dog was 1994, then, working backwards, 1982, 1970, 1958, 1946, 1934, 1922, 1910, and so on.

If anyone you know spends "much of their time in an advanced state of suspicious outrage," they may be Dog people, according to Suzanne White, the author of *The New Astrology*. Dog people also tend to be crusaders and seekers of justice, for their strong sense of righteous indignation motivates them to make things right. For example, President Clinton is a Dog person.

Among Dog people's finer qualities: consistency, heroism, respectability, faithfulness, loyalty, devotedness. (No wonder it's called the Year of the Dog.) They're devoted to family, firm friends, intelligent, highly moral, the last to give up on apparently hopeless causes (think of crusader Ralph Nader, Israel's Yitzakh Rabin, writer Joan Didion, former presidential hopeful George McGovern, commentator Bill Moyers). So far, so good.

But Dog people may also be critical, self-righteous, cynical, unsociable, and tactless—they're always picking bones with you. Donald Trump is a Dog person. So is Larry King. In fact, broadcasting seems to attract Dog people—besides King, there's Sam Donaldson, Connie Chung, Charles Kuralt, and Jim Lehrer.

Not to mention that moon-walking, sweet-singing, pick-of-the-litter-Dog Michael Jackson.

24

Howliday Dog Collar

From Valentine's Day to Christmas, this easy-to-make, "changeable" collar will be a howling success. You can buy the basic collar or make your own.

MATERIALS AND TOOLS

Fabric collar—or belt webbing to fit your dog's neck plus about 1" (3 cm)

Hook-and-loop tape in the same amount, plus 1/2" (1.5 cm) for each cut-out decoration (buy the adhesive kind of tape if you don't want to sew)

Felt in desired colors

Black felt (for backing decorations)

Strip of black felt, collar length (optional)

Acrylic paints in desired colors

Heavy-duty fabric glue

Sewing machine (optional)

Matching threads (optional)

"DOGS LAUGH, BUT THEY LAUGH WITH THEIR TAILS."
—MAX EASTMAN,
ENJOYMENT OF LAUGHTER

1

Sew or stick a strip of hook-and-loop tape to the right side of the collar or webbing—the decorations will stick onto this. If you're making the collar, sew a strip of black felt to the back of the webbing and sew or stick a 1" (3 cm) square of hook-and-loop tape to one end of the collar on the wrong side as a fastener.

2

Trace and cut out the patterns you want to use from page 114. From felt, make as many decorations as you need to fill the collar. Cut out and glue black felt on for backing on each decoration. Let glue dry. Glue or stick a square of hook-and-loop tape to each backing.

3

Embellish the decorations as you like, or copy the photo.

DESIGN
NANCY ASMUS

Santa Paws Suit

One of the special details of this Santa suit is its pocket, just right for carrying candy canes or small gifts for kids, guests, or clients—or treats for Christmas canine company. And the great thing about felt is, you don't have to hem it.

Before you begin:
The amount of fabric recommended makes a suit to fit a medium to large Santa, 40-45 pounds, but Holly Decker tells you how to measure your dog for the amount you'll need. All seams are 1/4" (1 cm).

MATERIALS AND TOOLS

1 yd. (.9 m) of red felt

1/4 yd. (23 cm) of white felt

1/4 yd. (23 cm) of black felt

15" (38.5 cm) of hook-and-loop tape

Cotton thread in red and white

Small amount of fiberfill

White glue or fabric glue

Sewing machine

Basic sewing equipment

> **"A REALLY COMPANIONABLE AND INDISPENSABLE DOG IS AN ACCIDENT OF NATURE. YOU CAN'T GET IT BY BREEDING FOR IT, AND YOU CAN'T BUY IT WITH MONEY. IT JUST HAPPENS ALONG."**
> —E. B. WHITE, "THE CARE AND TRAINING OF A DOG"

1

Refer to the drawing on page 120 as you measure your dog and custom fit your Santa suit. For A, the width of your suit, measure your dog around the widest part of the chest. For the length: Measure along the dog's back from collar to hip (measurement B-A), then measure from top of front haunch (shoulder) under the neck to the center neck (measurement C-D)—total these two measurements for the length (D-A). Double check all measurements before you cut the felt out, following the drawing. (Make sure the dog has enough breathing room to ho ho ho.)

2

To attach the trim: Cut a length of white felt 4" (10 cm) wide and as long as measurement A. To give the trim some body, fold it in half over fiberfill, then sandwich 1/2" (1.5 cm) of A edge between the edges (see drawing) and pin. With white thread, sew around ends of trim and sew trim to suit.

3

For collar trim: Cut a length of white felt 8" (21 cm) wide and equal to measurement C-C, across your dog's shoulders. Fold in half. Sew diagonally across folded corners to make the collar edge. Turn inside out and stuff loosely with fiberfill. Pin to collar edge (C-C), matching raw edges, then stitch.

4

For belt: Cut a length of black felt 1-1/2" (4 cm) wide by measurement A (in the photo, the belt doesn't run all the way around—this is your choice). Glue along waistline, per drawing. For the buckle, cut a 3-1/2" by 2" (9 by 5 cm) rectangle of black felt; cut a rectangle out of the center, about 1/2" (1.5 cm) from each edge. Glue the buckle over the center of the belt.

5

For the pocket: Cut a 3" by 4" (8 by 10 cm) rectangle of red felt and sew over belt, leaving the side nearest the buckle open.

6

For closings: Cut two pieces of hook-and-loop tape, each 3-1/2" (9 cm) long. Referring to the drawing, sew a piece to each under-neck closure at points D, so that they attach under the dog's chin. Cut two pieces of hook-and-loop tape, each slightly shorter than measurement E, and sew these to each side E so that the suit will attach under the dog's belly.

DESIGN HOLLY DECKER

TAIL-WAGGER TIP

London's Royal Humane Society, the first in the world, was founded in 1774 to benefit people, not animals. Its purpose was to teach people life-saving techniques so they could rescue people who were drowning. The American Society for the Prevention of Cruelty to Animals was founded in New York in 1866, ten years before the founding of the New York Society for the Prevention of Cruelty to Children.

Santa Beagle

Paper mache is not only one of the most inexpensive sculpting materials but one of the easiest and most forgiving. If Santa Beagle doesn't jingle your bells, how about Santa Boxer or Santa Poodle?

MATERIALS AND TOOLS

Cardboard

Instant paper-mache mix

Acrylic paints in desired colors

White glue

Matte spray sealer

Masking tape

Paper toweling

Antiquing medium

Paper plate

Purchased jingle bell, tiny teddy bear, tiny pine tree

Manicure set or sculpting tools

Paintbrushes

DESIGN
DOLLY LUTZ
MORRIS

1

Cut a cardboard oval 6" by 4" (15 by 10 cm) for the rug area. To build your armature, make a cardboard cone 7" (18 cm) tall with a 2" (5 cm) base for the dog shape; tape this to the center of the oval. For the bag armature, make a ball of paper toweling 1-3/4" (4.5 cm) in diameter; tape it to the oval beside the cone.

2

Work on a paper plate, so you can turn the piece around easily. Mix the paper mache according to package instructions. Cover the bag and cone with a 1/2" (1.5 cm) layer of mache, and cover the oval with a 1/4" (1 cm) layer, pressing in the details with your tools to make it look like a braided rug. Let dry.

3

To sculpt the dog: Create the back haunch from a 1-1/2" (4 cm) ball of mache; blend in well. (The more attention you pay to smoothing the mache well, the more attractive the finished Santa will be.) Form the back leg from a coil 2" by 3/8" (5 by 1.25 cm); blend in and shape with tools. Form the tail from a coil 3" by 1/4" (8 by 1 cm). For front legs, use two coils 2" by 1/2" (5 by 1.5 cm); blend in with tools and add small balls for front paws.

4

Round out the head with more mache mix; form the muzzle—about 1" by 1/2" (3 by 1.5 cm)—tapering at the nose; indent mouth with tools. Add and shape ears; add hat, fur trim, and ball at end of hat.

5

Shape the bag and give it a "lumpy" look; add the strap across Santa's chest. Shape the ball and bone in the bag—leave room for the jingle bell, bear, and tree to be added later. Make a paper mache bow around Santa's necks and shape and blend with tools. Let dry thoroughly.

6

Paint with acrylic paints. Let dry, then spray with sealer. Antique with antiquing medium to bring out the details and give the piece a mellow, aged look.

7

Finally, glue the bear, bell, and tree into the bag.

> "DOGS TEND TO STUDY US, BUT THEY MAKE NO CONCLUSIONS. THEY OBSERVE US, BUT THEY DO NOT JUDGE US. I SUBMIT THAT UNDER THIS KIND OF BENIGN SCRUTINY WE BEGIN TO FEEL COMFORTABLE ABOUT OBSERVING OURSELVES."
> —DANIEL PINKWATER, "A WALK WITH JACQUES"

Canine Christmas Tree

Deck the halls with "bows" of holly…and the tree with golden biscuits and dog treats. (Remember that the more you spray gold, the fewer the dog can eat—the paint's not edible.)

MATERIALS AND TOOLS

Artificial tree (this one's 2 feet high, or 62 cm)

Heavy dog dish (here, 8 inches, or 21 cm, across)

20 6" (15 cm) rawhide twists

12 5" (13 cm) rawhide chew sticks

60 (or more) medium dog biscuits with holes

1 yd. (.91 m) of red satin ribbon, 1-1/4" (3.5 cm) wide

8 yd. (7.2 m) of red satin ribbon, 1/4" (1 cm) wide

Gold spray paint

2 yd. (1.8 m) of 30-gauge wire

1 large rubber band

Fabric glue

Heavy scissors or wire cutters

DESIGN
JANET FRYE

30

1

Slip the rubber band on the tree trunk below the lowest branch. Hold the tree in the dish and lean the twists vertically against the trunk to serve as a stand. Secure with the rubber band near the top of the "stand." Spread out the lower limbs of the tree to cover the edge of the dish.

2

To make plain biscuit ornaments, thread a piece of wire about 4" (10 cm) long through the holes in two biscuits to make a "sandwich," then slide the sandwich onto the tip of a branch and twist the wire ends to secure it. Make twenty-five of these, or as many as you need to fill the tree.

3

Spray paint ten biscuits gold (or as many as you like). Wire some of these separately onto the tree.

4

Make bows with 18" (46 cm) lengths of the narrow ribbon and wire them onto the biscuits already on the tree.

5

To make stars, twist a piece of wire around the center of three chew sticks, one stick at a time. Tie bows around the centers of the stars, then secure by twisting the ends of the wire around a branch.

6

Loop the wider ribbon around the dish and secure with glue. Glue one gold biscuit (or many) onto the ribbon.

REMINDER: Do not let your dog have the gold-painted biscuits. Remove all wires from the other treats before giving them to your dog.

"FOR THOSE OF YOU ON THIS EARTH…WHO FIND PETS (OR CHILDREN) TO BE A VAST ANNOYANCE… LET ME WARN YOU THAT I HAVE IT FROM A PRETTY GOOD SOURCE…THAT SAINT PETER IS ACTUALLY A GUARD DOG, A STERN BUT NEVERTHELESS GOOD-HEARTED DOBERMAN PINSCHER, AND HE'S GOING TO WANT TO KNOW JUST WHAT IN THE WORLD IT WAS YOU THOUGHT YOU WERE TALKING ABOUT, BACK ON EARTH, WHEN YOU TALKED ABOUT LOVE."
—BOB SHACOCHIS,
"THE COMPANY OF CANINES"

"Bark! The Herald Angels Sing" Biscuit Ornaments

For decoration only, these charming, easy-to-make ornaments aren't edible by the time you get through dressing them up. They need to be out of reach—on a wreath, say, or a table-top tree.

MATERIALS AND TOOLS

Bone-shaped dog treats

All-materials glue (or hot glue, with hot-glue gun)

8" (21 cm) of silk ribbon, 1/8" (.5 cm) wide (for 3 ornaments)

Small dried flowers and berries

Scissors

1

Tie a ribbon around the treat and tie the ends at the top for a hanger

2

Glue on decorative materials—caspia, baby's breath, statice—then glue on accent flowers and berries. Add a ribbon bow.

"I HAVE CAUGHT MORE ILLS FROM PEOPLE SNEEZING OVER ME AND GIVING ME VIRUS INFECTIONS THAN FROM KISSING DOGS."
—BARBARA WOODHOUSE,
TELEGRAPH SUNDAY MAGAZINE

DESIGN
DOLLY LUTZ MORRIS

A yuletide treat that looks good enough to eat—to canine eyes—all tied up with a festive leash.

MATERIALS

8 4" (10 cm) natural beef bones

20' (6 m) cotton-web lead leash

2 small natural rawhide "baseballs"

6 mini rawhide chew bones

4' (1.2 m) of gold-wrapped wire

1 yd. (.9 m) of 18-gauge wire

1' (31 cm) of 30-gauge wire

"WHEN MY OLD DOG—COMPLETELY EXHAUSTED AFTER A FULL AND HARD DAY IN THE FIELD—LIMPS AWAY FROM HER NICE SPOT IN FRONT OF THE FIRE AND COMES OVER TO WHERE I'M SITTING AND PUTS HER HEAD IN MY LAP, A PAW OVER MY KNEE AND CLOSES HER EYES AND GOES BACK TO SLEEP, I DON'T KNOW WHAT I'VE DONE TO DESERVE THAT KIND OF FRIEND."
—GENE HILL, "THE DOG MAN"

1
Thread the 18-gauge wire through the center of the 8 large bones and form a wreath. Pull tightly and twist the ends together.

2
Loop the ends of the leash around the wreath and tie the excess into a bow at the top. Twist 30-gauge wire around the loop of the leash catch and secure it to the center of the bow.

3
Catch the strings from the baseballs into the leash catch.

4
Slip the rawhide bones under the leash "ribbon" in the center of each large bone.

5
Loop the gold wire around the wreath, centering it on the leash "ribbon," pull tightly, and twist the ends to form a loop at the top for hanging up the wreath.

REMINDER: Hang the wreath out of your dog's reach. Remove all wires before letting your dog loose on the wreath.

DESIGN
JANET FRYE

33

"We Three Pooches" Christmas Ornaments

One of the hidden beauties of these endearing polymer-clay ornaments is that they look professionally fired but you bake them in your oven, and they'll last forever. Of course you can custom match the star dogs to your own favorites.

MATERIALS AND TOOLS

Oven-bake polymer clay

Acrylic paints

Spray sealer

Paper clips

Gold thread

Gold wire (for angel)

Silk greens (for Labrador)

White glue

Antiquing medium

Manicure or sculpting tools

Small paintbrushes

"HOUSES ARE FOR PRIVATE LIVING, FOR FRIENDS, AND FOR DOGS."
—FRANÇOISE SAGAN

Poodle Angel

1

Shape the wings first, approximately 3-3/4" by 2" (9.5 by 5 cm); detail with tools. Add the robe, a triangle 3" by 2-1/2" (8 by 6.5 cm). Add sleeves, triangles 1-1/2" by 1-1/2" (4 by 4 cm); use tools to blend into robe and detail. Add tiny balls for paws, then add star.

2

For the head, begin with a 1" (3 cm) circle 1-1/4" (3.5 cm) thick; add muzzle and blend in. Add curly hair at top, detailing with tools. Add ears and texture with tools. Push a paper clip in the top of the head, leaving 1/8" (.5 cm) exposed for hanger.

3

To finish: Bake according to manufacturer's directions. Cool. Paint; allow to dry. Spray with sealer. When dry, antique with antiquing medium. Glue on gold wire circle for halo. Tie gold thread to paper clip for hanging.

Dalmatian/Stocking

1

Form a stocking about 2-3/4" (7 cm) long. For the dog's head, at the top of the stocking place a 1" (3 cm) circle 1/4" (1 cm) thick: detail with tools. Place two tiny circles under the head for paws, and a tiny circle for the muzzle. Add ears. Then add Santa hat, fur trim, and ball at the end of the cap: detail with tools. Push a paper clip in the top of the cap, leaving 1/8" (.5 cm) exposed for hanger.

2

Finish as for the Poodle Angel (without the halo).

Labrador/Hearth

1

Make the fireplace from a rectangle 2-3/4" (7 cm) tall by 3" (8 cm) wide. Create details of stone with tools. Add hearth rug from an oval 2-3/4" by 1" (7 by 3 cm). Next add stockings and logs.

2

Sculpt the dog on the rug, creating the body from an oval 1-1/2" by 3/4" (4 by 2 cm), then add back leg, tail, head, and ears. Blend in well with tools. Push a paper clip in the top of the fireplace, leaving 1/8" (.5 cm) exposed for hanger.

3

Finish as for the Poodle Angel, but after antiquing glue silk greens to the top of the fireplace.

DESIGN
DOLLY LUTZ MORRIS

35

Puttin' on the Dog

Sundog Lifeguard Ensemble

You can rest easy around the pool or at the beach with an alert canine lifeguard on duty, especially one in togs like these. (Some muscle-bound types—like Emmett here— may find the shorts a bit confining.)

MATERIALS AND TOOLS

Purchased cotton-knit shorts and tank top to fit your dog

Black acrylic paint

Scraps of red cotton and silver lamé

2" (5 cm) of hook-and-loop tape, 1" (3 cm) wide

Scrap of fusible web

Basic sewing equipment

Iron

1

Open up the back seam of the shorts to the crotch. Stitch around the entire opened seam to reinforce the knit. Sew half the hook-and-loop tape on one end of the waistband at the top of the opening, and the other half on the other end of the waistband, positioned so that the two pieces of tape will stick together to hold the waistband closed.

2

To decorate the tank top, paint small dots around the neckline to look like the chain for the whistle. Trace the red cross and whistle patterns (page 114) on fusible web. With a hot iron, press the red cross web paper side up onto the wrong side of the red cotton. Press the whistle web paper side up onto the wrong side of the silver lamé. *(Lamé melts easily, so be sure to use a press cloth.)* Cut out the motifs and peel off the paper. Again using a press cloth, iron the whistle and cross to the shirt. Appliqué the whistle and cross.

DESIGN
NANCY ASMUS

TAIL-WAGGER TIP

If you're a type-A personality with a stressful task to do, having your dog (instead of your partner) beside you may help you keep your cool. Research suggests that people who thrive in competitive, hard-driven life-styles are calmest when dogs are their only attendants (stress measured highest with spouses in the room)—maybe because dogs aren't judgmental. Try this when tax time rolls around, or the next time you're on the phone with a frustrating bureaucrat or meet with your insurance agent.

"YOU DIDN'T HAVE TO THROW A STICK IN THE WATER TO GET HIM TO GO IN. OF COURSE, HE WOULD BRING BACK A STICK IF YOU DID THROW ONE IN. HE WOULD EVEN HAVE BROUGHT BACK A PIANO IF YOU HAD THROWN ONE IN."
—JAMES THURBER, "SNAPSHOT OF A DOG"

Ecologically Correct Canine Fashion Sweaters

Recycle your old hand-knit sweaters into high-fashion garments for your dog—or raid used clothing stores and garage sales and come away with a potential wardrobe of outrageously chic recyclables. All you need are the simplest sewing skills—*no knitting required.*

MATERIALS AND TOOLS

Used sweater

Buttons (if you don't want to use the ones on the sweater)

Old pillowcase, towel, or cloth remnant

Basic sewing equipment or sewing machine

DESIGN
ENID SHOMER

Before you begin:
From an old pillowcase, towel, or other remnant, make a pattern that fits around your dog's middle, meeting at the center stomach. For a cardigan, make the pattern slightly wider between the front legs, to allow for the button band. Make slits at the front legs to attach sleeves to (or to hem, for a sleeveless sweater). To convert the people sweater into the dog sweater, take the people sweater apart either by cutting apart the seams at the sides and around the armholes, or by carefully clipping and pulling out the seams. (For cardigans for large dogs, you may not need to cut the people-sweater side seams at all, but simply remove the sleeves.) Enid Shomer found that knitwear does not unravel when cut if you sew it together right away.

Pullover

1

For small dogs, you can make the entire pullover sweater body from one sleeve, using the ribbing at the wrist for the ribbed collar and cutting slits for the legs according to your pattern. The original sleeve seam will become the stomach seam. The brown pullover in the photo is made from a people-sweater sleeve, with the original button band sewn onto the original wrist ribbing for a fashion collar, decorated with the original buttons.

2

For medium or large dogs, make a pullover from either the entire front of a people pullover or sew the two front pieces of a people cardigan together, matching your dog's pattern, to make back and stomach seams. Fit the pieces so the people-sweater ribbing becomes either the dog-sweater ribbing or the dog-sweater neck. Sew either with unraveled yarn from the sweater, using a large-eyed needle, or with regular sewing thread. You can cut the excess sweater parts away after you've sewn the seams.

3

If you now have ribbing at the neck, hem the bottom of the dog sweater—or sew on ribbing at the bottom from the people sweater, if you prefer.

4

If you have ribbing at the dog-sweater bottom and not at the neck, you can now either sew on ribbing from the people-sweater and/or measure a section of the people-sweater button band to sew loosely around the neck.

5

If you're making a sleeveless pullover, sew the seams around the leg slits, leaving them roomy enough to slip on and off your dog's front legs easily.

6

For any size dog, you can make "sleeves" by using either the bottom ribbing or sleeve ribbing from the people sweater as the dog sleeve ribbing. Cut pieces to fit your dog's front legs —make them roomy, since most dogs don't enjoy anyone fiddling with their toes to pull them through a tight cuff. Don't forget to allow for a seam at the side and the top. Sew each sleeve into a tube, right side in, so when you turn it right side out the seam will be on the inside. Sew the sleeves onto the body slits, right sides together.

"'A PARAKEET IS NICE,
LIKE A FEATHER ON A
HAT,' [MY GRANDMOTHER]
ALWAYS SAID...BUT
A DOG IS A MENSCH."
—ENID SHOMER,
"MR. AND MRS. FOO"

39

Cardigan

1

For small or medium dogs, make a cardigan from the people-sweater body—from the two front halves, if it's a cardigan. If you're starting with a pullover, use either the front or the back, and cut it up the middle. For the best fit, plan to sew the center back seam last. (The ceramic "dog buttons" on the light green cardigan in the photo came from the kids' section of a fabric-store button department.)

2

For very large dogs, make a cardigan by using an entire people cardigan (it will button under the dog's stomach). Unless the people sleeves happen to fall in the right spot for the dog's front legs, start by removing the sleeves and sewing those sleeve holes closed from the inside as invisibly as possible.

3

For any size dog: Fit the pieces so the people-sweater ribbing becomes either the dog-sweater ribbing or the dog-sweater neck. Based on your cardigan pattern (or your dog), sew hems at the center front. Sew on buttons along one side, and make buttonholes either by hand or machine opposite each button on the other side. Sew either with unraveled yarn from the sweater, using a large-eyed needle, or with regular sewing thread. (If you're using a people cardigan, simply button it up.)

4

Continue as for the pullover. Steps 3-6.

5

Unless you've been working from the entire people cardigan, you now need to sew the center back seam. For the best fit, simply try the sweater on your dog at this point and mark the seam for a comfortable fit. (Ask your dog how it feels.) Then sew the back seam, right sides together.

From Runaway and Throwaway to Service and Therapy

NEADS service dogs pose for a family portrait.

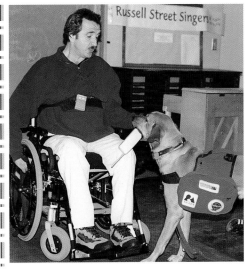

NEADS-trained service dogs retrieve dropped objects and bring their owners ringing telephones.

Bailey was a runaway, a mostly Labrador retriever with a sliced paw and a neck scraped raw by a rusty backyard chain. Natasha, an Akita, was a champion show dog whose hypothyroidism had made her too vicious to handle. LaToya, a three-year-old purebred pug, was found abandoned in a parking lot. All across the country every day, abandoned, neglected, and abused dogs are saved by rescue groups of all kinds. Humane societies. The National Education Assistance Dog Services, Inc. (NEADS). The Delta Society. Breed rescue groups, like Border Collie Rescue of Ohio and Delaware Valley Akita Rescue. They rescue the dogs no one wants— and then they rehabilitate them.

After about four years of work with her new owner, Regina Neumeister, Natasha became a certified therapy dog. "Therapy dogs have to be very calm," Neumeister said. "Natasha will pull a wheelchair, in harness. She visits nursing homes and a special school for children to let them pet her. Now I walk with a cane, and if I fall, Natasha will pull me up. My proudest moment was when she got her award for therapy dog. People say she and I are one spirit."

Like Natasha, most of the dogs NEADS trains to assist people were throwaways or runaways. The group has now trained more than five hundred assistance dogs—service dogs and hearing dogs. Hearing dogs learn to alert their nonhearing owners to smoke alarms, sirens, a baby's cry, or a ringing phone, according to Kathy Foreman, head trainer at the West Boylston, Massachusetts, headquarters. Among the tasks service dogs learn during their five months' training: to turn on light switches, go for help, open doors, carry colostomy equipment, bark on command for help.

Akita Rescue helped with Natasha's obedience training and therapy testing—among other tasks, the once-vicious dog had to heel and walk off-lead while people threw pots and pans around nearby, and react calmly to people with canes, walkers, crutches, and wheelchairs.

To contact these groups: NEADS, P.O. Box 213, West Boylston, MA 01583 (508/422-9064); Delta Society (therapy and service dogs), 289 Perimeter Rd., East, Renton, WA 98055 (1/800/809-2714); for breed rescue groups, call the American Kennel Club at 919/233-9767 or write Muttmatchers/HART, P.O. Box 920, Fillmore, CA 93015 (805/524-4542).

41

Salty-Dog Sailor Hat and Middy Collar

A seaworthy outfit even for canine landlubbers or for visionaries who, like Walter Mitty, dream of salt spray spattering the wheelhouse windows.

Before you begin:
All seams are 1/4" (1 cm). Refer to the patterns and size chart on page 115—a half yard of each fabric should be plenty for both projects.

MATERIALS

Blue broadcloth

Red broadcloth

1 yd. (.9 m) of white middy braid

Red double-fold bias tape: 36"-54" (92.5-138.5 cm) of wide tape and 38"-50" (97.5-128 cm) of regular-width tape

1-1/2" (4 cm) red pom-pom

White thermal fleece (for hat top)

Matching threads

Scraps of polyester filling

TOOLS

Sewing machine

Scissors

Ruler

Pencil

Iron

DESIGN
MARYN WYNNE AND LIZ FYE

The Sailor Hat (small and large)

1

Cut one blue broadcloth and one fleece piece from the hat-top circle pattern. Mark the center point on the blue broadcloth top where the pompon will go. Cut one blue broadcloth piece from the hat-bottom circle pattern with the circle cut out from the center. Sew one row of white middy braid around the top blue piece 3/4" (2 cm) from the edge. Set aside.

2

For the band: Cut two pieces of red broadcloth: small—1-3/4" by 12" (4.5 by 31 cm); large—1-3/4" by 14" (4.5 by 36 cm). Cut ear loops from the narrower bias tape: small—38" (1 m); large—50" (1.28 m). Sew the edges closed. Cut this length into two ear loop pieces and two tie pieces: small—ear loops 7" (18 cm) each, ties 12" (31 cm) each; large—ear loops 11" (28 cm) each, ties 14" (36 cm) each.

3

To sew the ear loops into the seam of the band in the middle of each side: small—2" (5 cm) apart; large—3" (8 cm) apart. To find the middle of each side, fold the bands in half; measure and mark 1/4" (1 cm) from each end where the seam will be. With the band still folded, fold once more: the center now meets your seam mark—mark this new fold.

Repeat for the other side. On each side of these mid-points, mark again: small—1" (3 cm) on each side; large—1-1/2" (4 cm) on each side. Pin the ear loops on these marks with the ends extending about 1/4" (1 cm) over the seam edge.

4

Sew the two band pieces lengthwise with right sides together (the ear loop should be inside, with the loop facing up from the seam). Sew the end seam together to form the band. Turn right side out, fold the band in half on the seam and press. Loops should be hanging from the bottom seam. Close the top of the band with a basting stitch 1/8" (.5 cm) from the edge.

5

To sew band to hat: Stuff the band tube with enough polyester filling to give it some body. Pin and sew the band to the cut-out circle of the hat bottom, right sides together. Turn right side out and press.

6

Finishing: Loop one end of the tape tie about 1" (3 cm) over each ear loop to form a small loop and sew this to itself. Knot the ends of the tape. Hand sew (or hot glue) the pom-pom to the center point on the hat top. (The ear loops fit around the dog's ears and tie under the chin.)

The Middy Collar

1

Cut two collar pieces from blue broadcloth. On one piece, sew middy braid 3/4" (2 cm) from the edge along the two side edges first, then along the bottom edge, crossing over the braid on the sides. With the collar pieces right sides together, sew along the outer edges of the collar, leaving neck curve open. Turn right side out and press.

2

Sew the wide bias tape to the neck edges (encase both edges), leaving 12" (31 cm) on each side for the ties, in this way: Finish one end of the tie by folding in the raw edge and stitching closed. Edge stitch the folded bias tape along one long side to make the tie; continue sewing the bias tape along the neck edge, then edge stitch along the other long side. Finish the second raw end as you did the first.

3

To form the neck band: Fold the bias tape to the inside of the collar. Top stitch about 1/2" (1.5 cm) along the neckline at each end to keep the bias tape in place. (Tie in a bow around the dog's neck.)

"ALTHOUGH OUR FATHERS AND MOTHERS VERY SENSIBLY NEVER PERMITTED A PUPPY TO COME INTO THE HOUSE, THEY MADE UP FOR THIS INDIGNITY BY ALWAYS CALLING THE PUPPY "SIR." IN THOSE DAYS A DOG DIDN'T EXPECT ANYTHING VERY ELABORATE IN THE WAY OF FOOD OR MEDICAL CARE, BUT HE DID EXPECT TO BE ADDRESSED CIVILLY."
—E. B. WHITE, "DOG TRAINING"

Vogue-Hound Victorian Vest and Hat

Recycle your old jeans to create this casual ensemble for the fashion-conscious and environmentally concerned canine. (This vest fits a medium-to-large dog; if necessary, adjust the pattern to your dog before you start cutting fabric.)

MATERIALS AND TOOLS

1 or 2 pairs of old jeans with back pockets

2-1/2 yd. (2.3 m) of ruffled eyelet lace

2-1/4 yd. (2 m) of pink ribbon, 3/4"-1" (2-3 cm) wide

3 pink buttons

8" (21 cm) of hook-and-loop tape

Denim hat

1/4 yd. (25 cm) of elastic (for hat)

2 ribbon roses or other decorations for hat

Fabric glue (optional)

Sewing machine

Basic sewing equipment

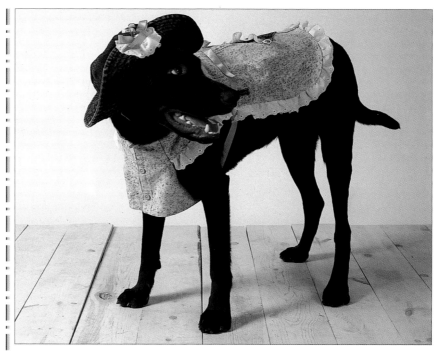

1

Refer to pattern, page 112. From the jeans fabric, cut out one vest on the fold and four straps. Cut one back pocket and two belt loops from the jeans.

2

Trim the pocket with lace at the top and a bow made from the ribbon. Sew to the vest where indicated on the pattern. Sew the belt loops to the vest where indicated.

3

Zigzag or serge the neck edge to prevent fraying. Turn back 1/2 inch (1.5 cm) and top stitch the neck edge.

4

Edge the long curved edge of the vest with lace, enclosing the raw denim edge.

DESIGN
CHERYL WEIDERSPAHN

5

To make straps, sew two sets, wrong sides together, with a 1/2-inch (1.5 cm) seam allowance, inserting ribbon ties where indicated on the pattern and leaving an opening to turn right side out. Clip curves and corners. Turn right side out and press. Slip stitch the opening closed.

6

Stitch hook-and-loop tape to overlap at center front. Sew on three buttons to decorate. Attach strap to vest (see photo).

7

Decorate the hat with 1/4 yard (about .25 m) of lace gathered to a circle, the two ribbon roses, and a ribbon bow (or your own preferred accents)—glue or sew these on. Stitch an elastic strap to go under your dog's chin, adjusting to fit. If you want to (or your dog requests it), cut holes in the hat for the dog's ears.

TAIL-WAGGER TIP

Although we now know that dogs can see in color (which is why dog-food commercials are no longer in black and white), they see mainly in pastel tints. They are also far better at seeing movement than detail—thus rabbits' protective "freezing" behavior.

"THE POSSESSION OF A DOG TODAY IS A DIFFERENT THING FROM THE POSSESSION OF A DOG AT THE TURN OF THE CENTURY, WHEN ONE'S DOG WAS FED ON MASHED POTATO AND BROWN GRAVY AND LIVED IN A DOGHOUSE WITH AN ARCHED PORTAL. TODAY A DOG IS FED ON SCRAPED BEEF AND VITAMIN B AND LIVES IN BED WITH YOU."
—E. B. WHITE, "DOG TRAINING"

Hair-of-the-Dog Hat

For this project, you start with a dog (if you're a purist) and end up with a hat—gather the dog hair, spin the yarn, crochet or knit the hat. Or you could simply crochet the hat. Or spin the yarn and make something else with it. Or just brush your dog and imagine the hat. Genna Miles chose to combine black sheep wool with white hair shed by Taiwaney, who is 85 percent wolf (pictured with her owner).

MATERIALS AND TOOLS

5 oz. of medium-thickness dog hair and black wool blended yarn or knitting worsted

Crochet hook, size H (UK 6, Int'l. 5)

Yarn needle

Wool cards (for spinning)

Drop spindle or spinning wheel

DESIGN
GENNA CLARK MILES

TAIL-WAGGER TIP

In the eighteenth century, people bitten by rabid dogs were advised to apply to their wound the hair of the dog that attacked them, as an aid to healing. Thus, the idea (probably put about by die-hard revelers) that "the hair of the dog that bit him" would cure one's hangover.

TO SPIN THE YARN

1

Begin with about 3 ounces of raw wool and about 2 ounces of dog hair. Card the wool and dog hair together to blend the fibers, first putting the wool on the cards and then adding as much dog hair as you can comfortably fit along the top of the wool. Brush together and create a good stack of carded wool.

2

Spin the fibers into yarn, aiming for a fairly tight twist. Skein the yarn, then wash it. Hang up the skeined, washed yarn to dry. Wind the dry yarn into a ball.

TO CROCHET THE HAT

Abbreviations (British equivalents in parentheses):
sc (dc) = single crochet (double crochet)
dc (tr) = double crochet (treble crochet)
tr (dtr) = triple crochet (double treble)
ch = chain
sp = space
st = stitch
sl = slip
Gauge: 4 sc (dc) = 1"; 3 rows sc (dc) = 1"

1

Ch 4—join with sl st to make a circle.

2

Ch 3—11 dc (tr) into center of circle (12 dc [tr]). Join with sl st. Ch 3. Do not turn.

3

1 dc (tr) into same st. *2 dc (tr) into next st. Repeat from * to end (24 dc [tr]). Ch 3. Do not turn.

4

Repeat Row 3 (48 dc [tr]). Ch 3.

5

Popcorn stitch: 3 dc (tr) into same st. Remove hook; insert in top of ch 3; reinsert hook into loop at top of last dc (tr); yarn over and pull through two loops on hook . *Ch 1; skip 1 st; 4 dc (tr) into next st. Complete popcorn as in Row 5. Repeat from * to end. End with sc (dc) in last st. Ch 1. Join to top of popcorn. Ch 1. Turn.

6

Sc (dc) into first sp. Ch 1. *Sc (dc) into next sp. Ch 1. Repeat from * to end. Ch 1. Join to top of sc (dc) with sl st. Ch 1. Turn.

7

Sc (dc) into first sp. Ch 1. *Popcorn into next sp. Ch 1. Sc (dc) into next sp. Ch 1. Repeat from * to end, ending with sc (dc). Ch 1. Join to top of sc (dc) with sl st. Ch 1. Turn.

8

Sc (dc) into same sp. *Ch 1. Sc (dc) into next sp. Repeat from * to end. Ch 1. Join to top of sc (dc) with sl st. Ch 3. Do not turn.

9

Tr (dtr) into next sp, 2 tr (dtr) into next sc (dc). Continue tr (dtr) to end, increasing every third st. Join with sl st. Ch 3.

10-13

Repeat Rows 5-8.

14

Tr (dtr) in each st, increasing every fifth st.

15

Repeat Row 5, without skipping st when you make last popcorn.

16-18

Repeat Rows 6-8. At end of Row 18, ch 1. Turn.

19

Sc (dc) into each st. Join with sl st. Finish off.

FOR THE RIBBING

1

Ch 6. Sc (dc) into third ch. Sc (dc) to end (5 sc [dc]). Ch 2. Turn.

2

Sc (dc) into back loop only of next sc (dc). Continue sc (dc) into back loops to end. Ch 2. Turn.

3

Repeat Row 2 for 60 rows or enough to go around circumference of hat. End off. Sew first and last rows together with yarn needle. Sew to bottom row of hat, working from the inside. For the last row: Working from outside the hat, attach yarn to ribbing with sl st. Ch 1. Working left to right, reverse sc (dc) into next st. Reverse sc (dc) all the way around. Join with sl st. Finish off.

Care of your hat: Hand wash and lay flat to dry.

> "HERE ONE DAY WOULD STAND A GIANT AMONG DOGS, POWERFUL AS A TIMBER WOLF, LITHE AS A CAT, AS DANGEROUS TO FOES AS AN ANGRY TIGER; A DOG WITHOUT FEAR OR TREACHERY; A DOG OF UNCANNY BRAIN AND GREAT LOVINGLY LOYAL HEART AND, WITHAL, A DANCING SENSE OF FUN. A DOG WITH A SOUL."
> —ALBERT PAYSON TERHUNE, "THE COMING OF LAD"

With a Bow (Wow) to Fashion

Maybe we've found one more way to categorize human beings: people who enjoy putting clothes on their dogs, and people who find people who put clothes on their dogs undognified.

A highly unscientific and unrandom survey shows that dressing—or dressing up—one's dog has nothing to do with the influences that shape human toggery, like economics, status, image, peer group, class, occupation, or living in New York City or Los Angeles. Breed and size count for something: We didn't find any big dogs dressed, except for various Christmas outfits on a few shepherds and retrievers, whose sheepish expressions suggest this is not their normal garb.

Small to medium breeds we've seen with their clothes on include Boston bulldogs, bull terriers, cocker spaniels, dachshunds, papillons, poodles, and one unidentified fluffy white mix in sunglasses.

One theory goes that people who dress their dogs view them as people, so of course they need clothes. *New York Times* feature writer Emily Prager puts forth "the much-espoused theory that dogs are child substitutes," along with "the lesser known one that children are dog substitutes." She adds a more obvious reason: "You can dress a dog. And simple physics tells you that if you can dress a dog, you will." But the most common motives for puttin' (clothes) on the dog in our totally unscientific survey were practicality, pleasure (the dog's), and philanthropy (the dog's and the owners').

PHOTO BY: LEVERT TUNGER

If you've fantasized about dressing your dog and are about ready to come out of the closet, you can buy almost any dog wear from pet catalogues (and check the back of dog magazines)—or of course you can start by making a few fashionable items yourself from the projects in this book. Off-the-rack sizes range from a Chihuahua's 4-6 to a toy poodle's 10, a boxer's 18, a rottweiler's 22 and a Great Dane's 36. (You measure in inches from the base of the neck to the base of the tail.)

Top left: Cindy and Andy Walker's miniature poodle, Zoe, gets cold in the Black Mountains of North Carolina without clothes. He wears a t-shirt (inside) and a parka (outside) in winter and also has a rain slicker, a cowboy hat and bandana, a pumpkin outfit for Halloween, and a sun visor at the beach.

Top right: Abbee, a toy poodle who lives in Tennessee with Teresa Smith, dresses up at the drop of a hat. "She's real cold natured," said Smith, who is an adherent of the child-substitute theory. "I don't have kids and I'm not married. She's got more clothes than I have"—including a wool chesterfield with a black velveteen collar.

Left: Sonnet, the fetching papillon of New York City poet Enid Shomer, "gets cold—and she really seems to enjoy wearing her clothes" (like this ear tidy and the sweaters in this book).

Dog-Walking Reflector Vest

A thoughtful, easy-to-make precaution for dogs outdoors, especially on walks and in the woods. Bright red or orange makes for high day-time visibility, and reflective tape makes your dog glow in the dark (sort of). This pattern is for small dogs; adjust pattern and materials to suit your dog's size.

MATERIALS AND TOOLS

1/2 yd. (.45 m) nylon rip-stop fabric

1-1/2 yd. (1.4 m) reflective tape, 1" (3 cm) wide

1/2 yd. (.45 m) belting, 3/4" or 1" (2 or 3 cm) wide (for straps)

Matching threads

12" (31 cm) hook-and-loop tape, 3/4" (2 cm) wide (adhesive backed, if you want to avoid sewing)

Sewing machine

Scissors

"WOULD I TAKE THE MORNING WALK, RELIGIOUSLY, DAY AFTER DAY AND YEAR AFTER YEAR, IF JACQUES WEREN'T WITH ME? DOUBTFUL. ALL MY LIFE I'VE PRIDED MYSELF IN NEVER KEEPING UP ANY KIND OF REGULAR EXERCISE PROGRAM."
—DANIEL PINKWATER,
"A WALK WITH JACQUES"

1
Cut two pieces of fabric according to the pattern (page 118). With wrong sides together, stitch the curved neck edge with a 1/4-inch (1 cm) seam allowance. Clip curves. Turn right side out. Topstitch neck edge. Zigzag around all other edges to prevent fraying.

2
Referring to pattern, top-stitch strip of reflective tape across back.

3
Cut belting in half. Zigzag all four raw ends to prevent fraying. Sew each piece of belting at the spot marked on the pattern.

4
Topstitch the remaining reflective tape to the three long edges of the vest.

DESIGN
CHERYL WEIDERSPAHN

5
Try the vest on your dog. Sew hook-and-loop tape under the neck to fit snugly (or if it's adhesive backed, stick it on), following the placement lines on the pattern.

6
Sew (or stick) hook-and-loop tape to belting straps to fit your dog snugly around the stomach.

Leader-of-the-Pack Tux Front and Bow Tie

De rigeur for a night on the town—tickets to "Cats," a benefit reading of Alan Ginsberg's "Howl," or a concert by famous canine crooner Bony Bennett, featuring "I Left My Hartz in San Francisco."

Before you begin:
Tux-front pattern is on page 113. All seams are 1/4" (1 cm). The bow tie's band holds the tux front on the dog's neck .

MATERIALS AND TOOLS

1/3 yd. (31 cm) of white broadcloth

White thread

12" by 12" (31 by 31 cm) of fusible interfacing

18" (46 cm) of grosgrain ribbon, 1-1/2" (4 cm) wide

24" (62 cm) of grosgrain ribbon, 5/8" (1.75 cm) wide

1-1/2" (4 cm) of hook-and-loop tape, 3/4" (2 cm) wide

Sewing machine

Scissors

Iron

The Tux Front

1

Fuse about 8" by 10" (21 by 26 cm) of interfacing to a piece of white broadcloth. From the tux-front pattern, cut one interfaced and one plain broadcloth piece. Right sides together, sew around both pieces, leaving an opening at the top of one side of the collar. Trim the seam along the curves and at the collar points. Turn right side out and press.

2

Top stitch along the top of the collar (this will also close the opening). Fold the collar points down over the shirt front as far as they will go; press. Take a few stitches along the outer side of the collar near the points to form a casing for the bow tie band.

The Bow Tie

1

For the band: Measure around the dog's neck, add 3" (8 cm), and cut a piece of the narrow ribbon to this measurement. Cut one 8" (21 cm) and one 10" (26 cm) piece of wide ribbon (for the bow) and one 2-1/4" (6 cm) piece of narrow ribbon (for the bow center). Sew the ends of the 8" (21 cm) piece together to form a loop. Repeat with the other two pieces of ribbon.

Turn each loop so that the seam is on the inside.

2

Place the smaller loop of wide ribbon on top of the larger one, matching center seams. Fold them in half lengthwise to slip them through the narrow center loop—it should now look like a bow tie. Slip one end of the band through the center loop behind the bow and adjust the bow's folds evenly—make sure all the seams are centered. Turn and sew a seam on each end of the band.

3

Cut the hook-and-loop tape in half lengthwise. Sew one strip on each end of the band, one on the outside and one on the inside. Insert the ends of the band through the collar points that you've stitched down. Pull through so that the bow tie is centered.

"WHEN I ADDRESS [MY DOG] I NEVER HAVE TO RAISE EITHER MY VOICE OR MY HOPES. HE EVEN DISOBEYS ME WHEN I INSTRUCT HIM IN SOMETHING THAT HE WANTS TO DO. AND WHEN I ANSWER HIS PEREMPTORY SCRATCH AT THE DOOR AND HOLD THE DOOR OPEN FOR HIM TO WALK THROUGH, HE STOPS IN THE MIDDLE AND LIGHTS A CIGARETTE, JUST TO HOLD ME UP."

—E. B. WHITE, "DOG TRAINING"

DESIGN
LIZ FYE AND MARYN WYNNE

Love My Dogma Sweater

The perfect design for really big dogs—you don't have to worry about stuffing their legs into sleeves, just drop it on and button! All you need to make this glamorous sweater are the most basic crocheting and knitting skills—and it's a great way for beginners to practice either of these.

Before you begin:

To make a striped sweater, as in the photo, divide total amount of yarn into three colors—or as many as you like. Attach a new color after you turn the hook at the end of a row, following the photo example. This amount of yarn crochets a sweater for a small dog; adjust the amount for your dog's size. (Stitch counts and measurements are for toy breeds; numbers in brackets are for medium and giant breeds.)

MATERIALS AND TOOLS

2-4 ounces of washable worsted-weight yarn

Tape measure

Crochet hook, size G (UK 7, Int'l. 4.5)—for a dense yarn, H (UK 6, Int'l. 5)

Knitting needles, size 7 (UK 7; Int'l. 4.5)

Corrugated cardboard 1-1/2" by 4" (4 by 10 cm)

Abbreviations (British equivalents in parentheses)

sc (dc) = single crochet (double crochet)

dc (tr) = double crochet (treble crochet)

hdc (htr) = half double crochet (half treble crochet)

ch = chain

yo = yarn over

1

Measure your dog from shoulder blades to just above the rump. (Don't make the sweater so long that it will get soiled when the dog relieves itself.)

2

Crochet a chain to fit your measurement. Work one row of dc (tr).

3

Pattern row 1: *Ch 3, turn. Alternate 1 back relief dc (tr), one front relief dc (tr) across row. In last st. work a hdc (htr). Pattern row 2: Ch 3, turn. Alternate 1 front relief dc (tr), one back relief dc (tr) across row. End with a hdc (htr).

Front relief stitch

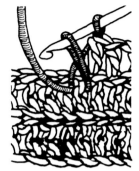

Back relief stitch

For relief stitches, work around the post of the stitch of the previous row: For front relief stitch, yo over hook, insert hook from right to left around the post of the indicated stitch at front of work. Yo, and draw through loop; yo, and continue as you would a dc (tr). The back relief stitch is identical except the hook is inserted at back of work.

4

Work in these two rows until blanket is wide enough to cover dog's back and ribs (but not its belly). Break off.

5

Work 2 rows sc (dc) around your blanket rectangle.

6

To make front belly bands: With knitting needle, pick up 14 [24, 44] sts. Work in k 2, p 2 rib for 3" (8 cm) [6" (15 cm), 9" (23 cm)]. (Measurements are approximate—make the ribbing length to fit your dog.) Bind off 2 st at beginning of next row and every other row three more times. Bind off the remaining stitches.

7

Make 2 pom-poms for buttons: For each. cut 10" (26 cm) piece of main yarn color and set aside. Wrap strands of yarn around cardboard about 20 times. Slide off, holding loops. Tie yarn bundle tightly in middle. Cut the loops, fluff, and trim. With main yarn color. attach to front belly band. evenly spaced, as buttons.

8

For the other belly band. repeat Step 6 on the opposite side of the rectangle. but instead of binding off. make two buttonholes when band is 4" (10 cm) [8" (21 cm). 12" (31 cm)] long: k 2. p 2. yo. k2 together. yo. k 2. p 2 for rest of row. Next row: k 2. p 2. Bind off.

9

Back belly bands: Join yarn about 2" (5 cm) [4" (10 cm). 8" (21 cm)] from back end of blanket and crochet 5 dc (tr) [10, 15]. Work narrow band in dc (tr) for 4" (10 cm) [6" (15 cm). 8" (21 cm)]. Buttonhole row: dc (tr). ch 3. skip 3 loops. dc (tr). For larger sizes: work ch 3 in middle of band. Work 2 more rows dc (tr). Break off. Button band: Attach yarn as before. Work 5 dc (tr). ch 2. turn. Work enough rows of dc (tr) to equal 1-1/2" (4 cm) [3" (8 cm). 5" (13 cm)]. Break off. Make and attach pompom as button.

"(1) JUSTICE AND
ORDER; (2) DOGS."
—EDITH WHARTON'S LIST
OF "RULING PASSIONS"

Pack-Your-Pooch Tote

Now you can tote your small dog on bike rides, keep your puppy close while waiting at the vet, and pack your short-legged dog along on those long hikes. Although Kim Tibbals designed the tote to be worn in front, it's adaptable.

Before you begin:
All seams are 1/2" (1.5 cm).

MATERIALS AND TOOLS

1/2 yd. of lining fabric, 45" or 60" (1.15 or 1.54 m wide)

1 yd. (.9 m) of tote fabric

2-1/2 yd. (2.28 m) of cotton woven strapping, 1" wide

16" (41 cm) heavy/sport zipper

2 1" (3 cm) plastic snap buckles

2 spring-loaded plastic barrel locks for drawcord

Sewing machine

Basic sewing equipment

Iron

DESIGN
KIM TIBBALS

1

From the tote fabric cut: three pieces (two fronts and one back), each 13" by 17" (33.5 by 44 cm), and eight tabs, each 3" by 4" (8 by 10 cm). Cut a piece of lining fabric 37" by 17" (95 by 44 cm). From the strapping cut two 15" (38.5 cm) straps and two 24" (62 cm) straps.

2

For the straps and tabs: Center the end of one strap sandwiched between two fabric tabs with their right sides together, aligning the raw end of the strap with the 3" (8 cm) ends of the tabs—pin through the three pieces.

Leaving the lower 3" (8 cm) edge open, stitch along the other three edges. Repeat with the other three straps.

3

Pull each tab over the end of its strap to turn it right side out.

4

For the back: On the right side of the fabric, measure 11" (28 cm) down each long side of the back piece and pin one waist tab (with its 15" [38.5 cm] strap) at each position. Stitch, then reinforce by stitching 1/4" (1 cm) into the seam allowance.

5

For the tote body: Right sides together, pin one front piece along each long side of the back piece and stitch. Open the three-part piece and press flat.

6

For the zipper: Right sides together, machine baste the two front pieces together along the long sides. Press flat. Position the zipper over this basted seam (on the seam allowance side), leaving a 1/2" (1.5 cm) margin at top and bottom. (Zipper tab should face the seam.) Hand baste the zipper in place. Pin together the bottom edges of the tote with zipper seam at center front. Stitch.

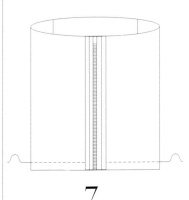

7

To square off the corners: On the wrong side, open the seam at both bottom corners of the tote and press flat, centering the seam (see drawing). Measure 3" (8 cm) down the seam from one corner and mark. Draw a line perpendicular to the seam, crossing that mark, and stitch on this line. Repeat for the other corner. Turn the tote right side out.

8

For the lining: Baste the two short sides together, right sides together. Right sides together and the basted seam centered, stitch across the bottom edge, leaving a 7" (18 cm) opening in the center. Repeat Step 7 to square the lining corners.

9

For the shoulder straps: Pin the shoulder tabs to the back of the tote, 1/2" (1.5 cm) toward the center from each side seam, the raw edges of the tabs even with the top raw edge of the back. Baste. Stitch a 1/4" (1 cm) seam.

10

To join tote and lining: With lining turned wrong side out, slip the tote inside the lining with center seams aligned and top edges even. Pin. Stitch through all thicknesses. Pull the entire bag through the opening in the bottom to turn it right side out. Push the lining into place inside the bag.

11

Press the top seam thoroughly. Align the center seam of the zipper with the center seam of the lining and pin. Beginning 3/4" (2 cm) down from the top, stitch along both sides of the zipper 1/4" (1 cm) from seam.

12

Create a zipper casing by stitching 3/4" (2 cm) around the top edge of the bag. Pin a large safety pin to one end of the cord and

feed it through the casing. Slip barrel locks on each cord end. Knot cord ends and trim.

13

To finish straps: Finish the waist straps by slipping the prong portion of a buckle onto each strap and threading it back through the buckle lock. Double over raw edges of straps and stitch. Finish the shoulder straps by slipping the remaining portion of the buckle onto each strap and doubling the strap back to

overlap about 3" (8 cm). Fold under raw edge and stitch close to edge. Stitch again halfway between that seam and the buckle. Finis.

"THERE IS NO PSYCHIATRIST IN THE WORLD LIKE A PUPPY LICKING YOUR FACE."
—BERN WILLIAMS

Top-Dog Leash Rack and Shelf

You can recreate this striking canine checkerboard or custom make your canine's hat, coat, and leash rack with the dog's own distinguished and distinctive silhouette.

MATERIALS

Acrylic paint in desired colors

Carbon paper

Pencil

Masking tape

Polyurethane finish

Purchased shelf with pegs, 5-1/4" by 16" (13.5 by 41 cm) or

> *4-1/2" by 3/4" (11.5 by 2 cm) pine, 16" shelf (41 cm) and 14-3/4" rack (38 cm)*
>
> *2 pegs, 2-3/4" (7 cm)*
>
> *2 wood screws, 1-1/4" (3.5 cm)*

TOOLS

Paintbrushes

Sandpaper

Saw and drill (if you're building the shelf yourself)

DESIGN
DOLLY LUTZ MORRIS

1

To build the rack/shelf: Attach shelf to rack by screwing wood screws through the top of the shelf into the top edge of the rack. Drill for pegs, centering holes 3" (8 cm) from each side and 1" (3 cm) up from the bottom of the rack. (Don't glue pegs in yet.) Sand.

2

For built or purchased rack/shelf: Paint shelf and pegs brown, as in the photo, or create your own color scheme. Divide the bottom into eight equal sections and use making tape to mask off areas for crisp lines as you paint; paint the squares as shown in your choice of colors. Let dry.

3

Using the silhouette dog patterns on page 119 or your own drawings, transfer the patterns onto the rack with carbon paper. Paint the silhouettes and allow to dry.

4

Glue pegs into predrilled holes. Seal with two coats of polyurethane finish.

"THEN WHO SHALL PICTURE THE URGENCY OF A BOY, RUNNING, AWKWARDLY, WITH A GREAT DOG IN HIS ARMS RUNNING THROUGH THE VILLAGE?...OR WHO SHALL DESCRIBE THE HIGH TONES OF A VOICE— A BOY'S VOICE, CALLING AS HE RUNS UP A PATH: 'MOTHER! OH, MOTHER! LASSIE'S COME HOME! LASSIE'S COME HOME!'"
—ERIC KNIGHT, "LASSIE COME-HOME"

Woman Bites Dog

Just seeing if you were paying attention. Actually, in the United States every year, people report more than two million dog bites—that is, dog bites person. In a recent year, 2,700 of those bitten were letter carriers, a more risky profession than advertised.

What can you do to help make sure your dog never adds to these statistics? The Humane Society of the United States suggests that you:

● Spay or neuter your dog. Unneutered dogs are more likely to bite.

● Enroll your dog (and yourself) in obedience training, where your dog can learn proper behavior and you can learn how to control your dog in any situation.

● When a delivery person (or any stranger) comes to your home, keep your dog inside, away from the door in another room or on a leash.

● Don't let your child take a package or mail from a delivery person if your dog is present. The dog's instinct is to "protect" the family.

You can avoid becoming a dog-bite statistic yourself by taking some precautions:

● Don't run past a dog (this makes you look like prey, and the dog will want to give chase).

● If a dog threatens you, don't scream. Avoid making eye contact, try to remain motionless until the dog leaves, then back away slowly until the dog is out of sight.

● Don't approach a dog you don't know, especially one that's tied or confined.

● Always let any dog to whom you're introduced see you and sniff you before you pet it.

If you want to celebrate another bite-free year, for yourself and your dog, National Dog Bite Prevention Week is June 12 - 17.

New Leash on Life...and Collar

The beauty of making your own leash and collar, of course, is that you can coordinate it perfectly with either your dog's or your own wardrobe. This collar fits an average-to-large dog.

MATERIALS AND TOOLS

3 yd. (3 m) of nylon strapping, 1" (3 cm) wide

3-1/4 yd. (3.25 m) of braid trim, 1/2"-3/4" (1.5-2 cm) wide

Double-sided fusible webbing

1" (3 cm) plastic snap buckle

1" (3 cm) plastic D ring

1" (3 cm) compatible stainless swivel hook

White craft glue

Iron

Sewing machine

Basic sewing equipment

DESIGN
KIM TIBBALS

1

For the leash, cut 7' (2.1 m) each of strapping and of trim; for the collar, cut 24" (62 cm) of strapping and 30" (77 cm) of trim. With a hot iron, fuse the trim to one side of the leash. When you fuse the braid trim to the front of the collar, you will have 6" (15 cm) extra to wrap around one end and fuse to the back of the collar. Stitch along the long edges of the trim.

2

To make the leash's hand grip: Fold over about 9" (23 cm) of one end and stitch across both pieces 1/2" (1.5 cm) from the raw end and again 2" (5 cm) from the raw end. Seal the raw edge with glue.

3

Thread the other end of the leash through the swivel hook and fold the end back on itself about 2-1/2" (6.5 cm). Stitch together 1" (3 cm) from swivel hook and again 2" (5 cm) from the hook. Trim the raw edge to 1/2" (1.5 cm) and seal with glue.

4

Slip the receiver portion of the buckle onto the end of the collar without the doubled over trim, trim side up. Fold about 3" (8 cm) of the end back onto itself. Stitch across both pieces 1" (3 cm) from

the buckle. Slip the D ring between the pieces and stitch on the other side of the ring, securing it in place. Trim the remaining raw edge to 1/2" (1.5 cm) and seal with glue.

5

Slip the other end of the collar through the other portion of the buckle and back on itself through the self-lock. Adjust size as needed.

"MOST DOGS ARE EARNEST, WHICH IS WHY MOST PEOPLE LIKE THEM. YOU CAN SAY ANY FOOL THING TO A DOG, AND THE DOG WILL GIVE YOU THIS LOOK THAT SAYS, MY GOD, YOU'RE RIGHT! I NEVER WOULD HAVE THOUGHT OF THAT!"
—DAVE BARRY,
"EARNING A COLLIE DEGREE"

TAIL-WAGGER
TIP

● When training your
dog, never jerk the
leash; flick it like a
towel.

● Leash train your dog
not to jump on people—
don't yell or knee.

Warp-and-Woof-Woof Beaded Collars

These elegant collars make wonderful beginning projects for beading on a loom, and you know for sure someone's going to wear them. (You make your own simple loom.)

MATERIALS AND TOOLS

Nylon dog collar

Assorted #11 seed beads, one pack per color

Beading thread (O weight)

Multipurpose glue (with a good bond for variety of surfaces)

Beading needles for #11 beads

12" by 15" (31 by 38.5 cm) wooden picture frame or stretcher frame and push pins (for beading loom)

1

Make your own beading loom for this project by positioning four push pins evenly spaced on two sides of the wooden frame. Wrap your beading string around one side of the frame enough times to secure it. Then begin wrapping the string around the pins, back and forth across the frame four times, ending with sixteen strings—four warp strings per pin. (If you're designing your own collar, be sure to thread your beading loom with one thread more than your design calls for.) At the end, wrap the thread around one side of the frame again and tie it to the beginning of the thread to secure it. Whenever you're knotting the thread, use a square knot when possible (right over left and under, left over right and under).

2

Refer to the graphed design on page 111 or graph your own design on beadwork paper. Reading the graphed design from left to right, you'll string beads from each row of the design onto your needle, one at a time.

3

Thread your needle and knot the other end of the thread to the last warp thread on the left. (Nancy McGaha likes to hold the loom in her lap vertically, so that it's easy to work around.) Following the graph, string the first row of beads onto your needle. Hold the entire threaded row behind the warp threads on your loom, then pop the beads into place so that a warp thread lies between each bead. (Once you've done this row, it's a piece of cake. It's the hardest row because you're separating the threads.)

4

Now send the needle back through the holes in the beads, traveling over the top of the warp threads and thus weaving the beads in place.

5

Refer to the graph and thread the second row of beads. Repeat the same process for each row.

6

To finish: When you've woven the last row of beads, to lock your thread: Weave only your thread as for the next to last row, from left to right, then as for the last row from right to left— you've made a circle of thread.

7

To tie off: Cut the warp threads close to the push pins to leave yourself as much thread as possible to work with when tying off. Tie the warp threads together, two or four at a time, in square knots. Clip excess thread.

8

To attach to collar: Fold knots under and glue the beaded work to the collar. When the glue is dry, remove any excess.

DESIGN
NANCY MCGAHA

TAIL-WAGGER TIP

In hot weather, attach a "licker" (you can buy them at the pet store or make one) to an outdoor faucet that your dog can reach. To get fresh water, your dog simply licks the device. (To encourage its use at first, put a bit of sugar on the licker.)

"I OWN TWO DOGS, AND THEY BOTH HAVE BEEN TRAINED TO RESPOND IMMEDIATELY TO MY VOICE. FOR EXAMPLE, WHEN WE'RE OUTSIDE, ALL I HAVE TO DO IS ISSUE THE FOLLOWING STANDARD DOG COMMAND: 'HERE ERNEST! HERE ZIPPY! C'MON! HERE! I SAID COME HERE! YOU DOGS COME HERE RIGHT NOW! ARE YOU DOGS LISTENING TO ME? HEY!!!' AND INSTANTLY BOTH DOGS, IN UNISON, LIKE A PRECISION DRILL TEAM, WILL CONTINUE TROTTING IN RANDOM DIRECTIONS, SNIFFING THE GROUND."
—DAVE BARRY, "YELLOW JOURNALISM"

"Out, Damned Spot" Towel

Just what a damp pooch needs after a walk, on days when it's raining cats and dogs. You'll find the compressed sponge and fabric medium (which keeps dried paint flexible and prevents it from cracking or growing brittle) at craft stores.

MATERIALS

1 sq. yd. (90 sq. cm) of terry cloth or a purchased towel

2 shades of brown acrylic fabric paint

Fabric medium

Sponge, compressed paper-thin

Glue

Cardboard scrap

Alphabet stencil

Scraps or 1/8 yd. (11 cm) of cotton print (for letters)

Scraps or 1/8 yd. (11 cm) of fusible web

Grommet (optional—for hanging)

TOOLS

Basic sewing equipment
Sewing machine (optional)
Iron

DESIGN
NANCY ASMUS

62

1

If you're not using a purchased towel, draw a stitching line at each corner of the terry cloth, using a rounded object like a bowl or plate as a pattern. Serge or overcast all edges.

2

Draw a paw pattern on paper and glue it to the sponge temporarily, then cut out each piece of sponge, dampen it, and allow it to expand and dry completely. Glue the pieces of the sponge in the paw pattern to a piece of cardboard and let dry.

3

Mix fabric medium with each of the paints. Dip the sponge in paint and randomly stamp paws on one corner of the towel. Allow to dry completely.

4

Trace letters from the stencil onto the fusible web to spell out "Wipe Your Paws" or another phrase of your choice—or your dog's name. Press the letters to the wrong side of the letter fabric with a dry hot iron. Cut out the letters, peel off the paper backing, and arrange the letters

on the towel, web side down (if you're going to hang the towel from its other corner, be sure the letters will be right side up when it's hanging). Bond the letters to the towel with a dry hot iron, then appliqué, if you wish.

5

Optional: Place a grommet in the opposite corner (follow directions on the package).

TAIL-WAGGER TIP

Get your puppy used to having her feet handled, so she won't grow up terrified of nail trimming. And don't try to trim all her nails in one sitting.

"I COULDN'T TELL YOU HOW MANY TIMES OUR SMALL PACK HAS MADE ITS WAY ACROSS THE FENCED ACRE WE HAVE FOR THEM....AND YET EVERY MORNING WHEN THEY CHARGE OUT THE BACK DOOR AND INTO THE FIELD, IT'S WITH THE WIDE-EYED AMAZEMENT OF CORTEZ ON A PEAK IN DARIEN. WHAT NEW WONDER WAITS IN STORE? WHAT NEW OUTRAGE?"
—STEVEN BAUER,
"TAKE THAT, WILL ROGERS"

Pooch Pack

Give your dog the pleasure of toting your keys, money, or ID in a dapper, waterproof collar pack. This one fits a large dog—but it's easy to cut the pattern down for smaller pack animals. The D-rings allow you to adjust the collar length.

MATERIALS AND TOOLS

3/4 yd. (68 cm) of belting or nylon webbing 1 inch (3 cm) wide (for collar)

2 1" D rings

1/4 yd. (23 cm) of vinyl fabric in your dog's favorite color

1 9" (23 cm) zipper

Matching threads

Sewing machine

Basic sewing equipment

1

Secure the cut ends of the belting with a machine zig-zag to prevent fraying. Slide both D rings onto one end, fold back, and stitch securely.

2

Refer to the pattern on page 114 to cut two bones from the vinyl. Stitch one bone to the collar on the stitching lines.

3

Place the zipper, face down, on the back of the other bone. Tape or pin in place. Stitch through both sides of the zipper tape. Carefully slit vinyl between the two stitching lines (watch out for the zipper!) to expose the zipper. Trim off any zipper tape on the ends.

4

Place the bones wrong sides together and stitch together close to the edges. (Take care not to catch the collar in this stitching.)

"MORNING WALK. OUTSIDE AT LAST, WE RETRACE OUR PATHS AROUND ONE OR ANOTHER BLOCK, ROMP THROUGH ONE OR ANOTHER FIELD TO RETRIEVE AND LEAVE MESSAGES ON ALL THE CANINE ANSWERING MACHINES POSTED THROUGHOUT THE NEIGHBORHOOD."
—MICHAEL J. ROSEN, *DOG PEOPLE*

DESIGN
CHERYL
WEIDERSPAHN

Puppy Love Toddler Sweat Suit

When a puppy can't keep its paws off you. it must be love. You can adapt this project using any child's pattern and just about any fabric.

MATERIALS AND TOOLS

Toddler pattern for sweat suit

1 yd. (.9 m) of patchwork flannel

1/2 yd. (46 cm) of flannel in a coordinating solid color

1 yd. (.9 m) of matching ribbing or elastic

Fabric paint

Fabric medium (from a craft store)

Cotton-tipped swabs

Buttons to cover

Matching thread

Iron

Sewing machine

"SHOPPING FOR A PUPPY HAS NEVER PRESENTED MANY PROBLEMS FOR ME, AS MOST OF THE PUPPIES AND DOGS THAT HAVE ENTERED MY LIFE...WERE NOT THE RESULT OF A SHOPPING TRIP BUT OF AN ACT OF GOD."
—E. B. WHITE, "DOG TRAINING"

1

Pin pants and sleeves pattern to patchwork plaid fabric and cut out. Pin top front and back to solid-color fabric and cut out. Don't place front on a fold, as it will be open; add 1" (3 cm) on each side of center front for facing.

2

Mix paint with fabric medium and use cotton swabs dipped in paint to form dog paws (practice on scraps first!). Draw a dog paw in every solid-colored square on the pants and sleeves. Cover buttons with solid flannel scraps and paint dog paws on each. Let all the paint dry completely.

3

Follow pattern instructions to make pants and top—finish ankles and wrists with either elastic or ribbing.

4

Turn under 1" (3 cm) on both sides at center front and serge or top stitch all the way around collar, front, and bottom edges. Sew two buttonholes on one side of front. Sew your "paw" buttons to correspond on other side.

DESIGN
NANCY ASMUS

TAIL-WAGGER TIP

According to behaviorist Desmond Morris, in the wild, during puppies' "prehunting" phase, adult dogs bring hunks of meat for them to chew on. No wonder that when humans leave things lying around on the ground—like slippers or books—during this stage of puppy growth, puppies view them as welcome gifts. Scolding a puppy for chewing these gifts must be "both puzzling and hurtful" for a puppy who's only trying to adjust to its "human pack."

Ethan Howlin' Four Poster

Here's the perfect sleeper for the dog-tired canine who prefers the traditional look of well-polished mahogany. Don't be intimidated by the fine-furniture style—you can pick up all the parts at your local home-improvement store, where they should be glad to cut the proper wood lengths for you.

MATERIALS

- 1/4" (1 cm) plywood, 18" by 21-1/2" (46 by 55 cm)
- 1" by 4" (3 by 10 cm) pine: 2 18" (46 cm) lengths (for side rails) and 23" (59 cm) (for footboard)
- 1" by 12" (3 by 31 cm) pine, 23" (59 cm) (for headboard)
- 4 turned posts
- 2 small carved appliqués
- 1 large carved appliqué
- 3/4" by 3/4" (2 by 2 cm) pine: 2 15" (38.5 cm) lengths and 2 21" (54 cm) lengths (for supports)
- Decorative molding: 2 16-1/4" (41.5 cm) lengths and 1 23" (59 cm) length
- 1" and 1-1/4" (3 and 3.5 cm) finish nails
- 1-1/4" (3.5 cm) wood screws
- 1/2" (1.5 cm) brads
- Sandpaper (fine)
- Wood glue
- Wood filler (optional)

TOOLS

- Yardstick or straight edge
- Jigsaw
- Compass
- Rasp, heavy file, or router with 1/4" (1 cm) roundover bit
- Hammer
- Nail set
- Screwdriver

1

For the headboard: Lay the headboard piece on a flat surface. Lay your straight edge along the right edge of the board and draw a line that extends 3" (8 cm) beyond the board top (see drawing). Make a mark 2-1/2" (6.5 cm) up that line from the edge of the board. Repeat on the left side. With the compass set at a 5" (13 cm) radius, set the compass point on each mark and draw the curve on each top corner of the headboard. Cut out the corners with the jigsaw.

2

For the footboard: Measuring along the top of the footboard, mark 4-1/4" (11 cm) in from each upper corner (see drawing). Measure down 1" (3 cm) on each side edge and draw a line across the entire board connecting those two marks. With the compass set at a 1" (3 cm) radius, draw two curves connecting that line with the marks at the top of the board. With the jigsaw, cut the center waste section out between the curves.

3

Using the file, rasp, or router, round over, inside and out, the top edge of each side rail and the footboard, stopping an inch (2.5 cm) short of each end. If you wish, round the top edge and 2" (5 cm) down each side of the headboard.

4

To attach supports for plywood sheet: Center one 15" (38.5 cm) piece flush with the inside bottom edge of each side rail, and 21" (54 cm) pieces flush with the inside bottom edge of the headboard and footboard. Glue and attach with 1" (3 cm) finish nails.

5

To make the bed frame: With the side rails overlapping the headboard and footboard, nail the four pieces of the frame together

DESIGN
MARK STROM

"I COULD NEVER TAKE DOGS FOR GRANTED....THEY WERE JUST ANIMALS,
AFTER ALL, AND IT SEEMED TO ME THAT THEIR MAIN PREOCCUPATION
OUGHT TO BE IN SEEKING FOOD AND PROTECTION; INSTEAD THEY DISPENSED
A FLOW OF AFFECTION AND LOYALTY WHICH APPEARED TO BE LIMITLESS."
—JAMES HERRIOT,
JAMES HERRIOT'S DOG STORIES

69

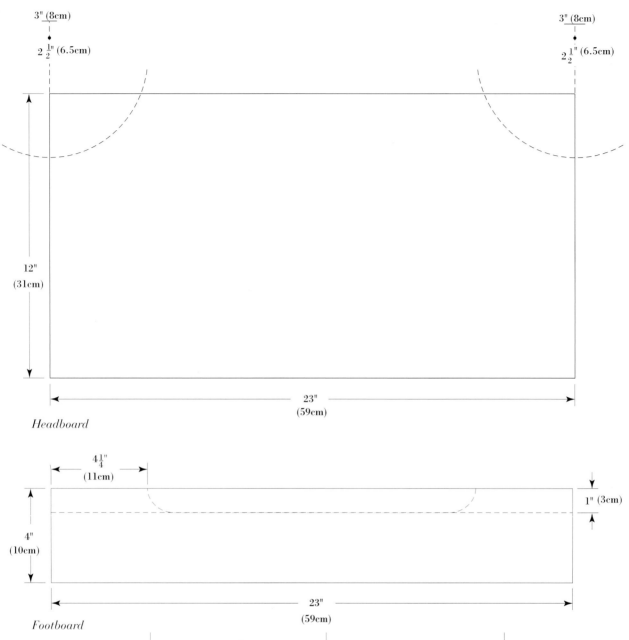

3" (8cm)

2 $\frac{1}{2}$" (6.5cm)

3" (8cm)

2 $\frac{1}{2}$" (6.5cm)

12"
(31cm)

23"
(59cm)

Headboard

4 $\frac{1}{4}$"
(11cm)

1" (3cm)

4"
(10cm)

23"
(59cm)

Footboard

with 1-1/4" (3.5 cm) nails. Be sure the supports are on the lower inside edge of each of the four sides. (You should now be able, when the bed is finished, to set the plywood on the supports inside the frame; you don't need to nail it.)

6

Attaching the posts: Position the posts outside the frame, one at each corner and even with the headboard and footboard. Allow about a 2" (5 cm) space between the bottom of the bed frame and the floor. From inside the frame, attach each post with two screws through the side rails.

7

Finishing touches: Attach the decorative moldings along the bottom edges of the side rails and footboard using glue and 1" (3 cm) nails. Attach the large appliqué to the headboard and small ones to the footboard using glue and 1/2" (1.5 cm) brads. Use the nail set to countersink all nails

that show, then fill the recesses with wood filler if you wish. Sand all surfaces. Finish as you like—for this project, Mark Strom used a mahogany stain and a polyurethane finish.

Hungry Dogs Floorcloth

When is a rug a painting? When it's a floorcloth. This colorful project happens in two phases: First you make the floorcloth, then you decorate it. (A floorcloth is a painted canvas rug sealed with varnish, happy on any hard floor surface.)

MATERIALS

#10 canvas, 34" by 42" (87 by 108 cm)

Acrylic gesso

Flat white exterior latex paint

Acrylic tube paints in desired colors for design

Flat exterior latex paints in desired background colors (here, yellow and purple)

Matte medium (from craft store)

Acrylic sealer or varnish

Clear bowling-alley-type paste wax

Liquid rubber backing

White polyester thread

Painter's masking tape

Paint conditioner

TOOLS

Straight edge and right angle for measuring and marking

Sewing machine with heavy-duty needle

Brushes

Soft-bristle artist's brush, medium

Roller (for gesso) with medium rough cover

Foam roller (for rubber backing)

2 roller pans

Sponge

Cheesecloth (for applying paint)

Making the Floorcloth

1

Prepare the raw canvas with acrylic gesso, rolled on with a roller.

2

Over the gesso, paint a coat of flat white exterior latex paint.

3

Mark the canvas into a rectangle that measures 30" by 38" (77 by 97.5 cm); make a dotted line 5/8" (1.75 cm) outside the rectangle.

4

With your sewing machine set on a long stitch, hem the floorcloth using a new heavy-duty needle and white polyester thread.

5

Apply a second coat of flat white exterior latex paint over the entire painted surface.

Decorating the Floorcloth

1

Tape off a 6" (15 cm) border on the top and bottom. With damp balled-up cheesecloth, rub on yellow exterior latex paint (or the color of your choice), thinned with paint conditioner, using a circular motion. Let dry. Tape around the center area and follow the same procedure, using purple latex paint (or another color). Let dry.

2

Using your own or children's drawings for inspiration, pencil dogs in various sizes along the border top and bottom, then paint in bright acrylic colors, using the soft-bristle brush. Let dry. Add flowers and spirals in the center area. Let dry. Use paint pens to add detail to dogs. Finish off border with a thin line in a contrasting color. Let dry. Add dots on the line. Let dry.

3

Wipe the dry painted surface with a clean, damp sponge to remove any dirt. Apply a coat of acrylic sealer. Let dry. Repeat with three to five more coats of sealer, until the surface is smooth.

4

Apply a coat of clear bowling-alley-type paste wax on the painted surface. Let dry and buff to a sheen with a clean, soft rag.

5

Apply a coat of nonskid rubber backing to the back of the floorcloth.

Care of your floorcloth: First vacuum, then clean with a damp mop or sponge and soapy water (or white vinegar and water). Rinse with clear water and wipe dry. Apply a thin coat of bowling-alley wax; buff. Don't fold or bend the floor cloth or put it in the washing machine. To move or store your cloth, roll it around a rigid-core cardboard tube or plastic pipe.

For more floorcloths, check out Kathy Cooper and Jan Hersey's new book, *The Complete Book of Floorcloths,* from Lark Books.

"MOST DOGS ARE TERRIBLY INFORMAL CREATURES. THEY DO THINGS IN COMPANY THAT WE WOULD ONLY DO IN PRIVATE. IN FACT, THEY DO THINGS IN COMPANY THAT WE WOULD NOT DO, EVEN IN PRIVATE—THIS IS TRUE OF ME ANYWAY, AND I HOPE OF THE READER."
—DANIEL PINKWATER,
"A WALK WITH JACQUES"

DESIGN
KATHY COOPER

73

Where's-the-Fire Afghan

MATERIALS AND TOOLS

6 oz. (170 g) of scarlet worsted-weight yarn*

6 oz. (170 g) of silver worsted-weight yarn*

27" (69 cm) circular knitting needle, size 10-1/2 (UK 2, Int'l. 7) or the size you need to achieve the correct gauge

Darning needle

*Suzann Thompson designed this afghan for Monsanto's Designs for America Program; it's knitted with Lion Brand Jiffy yarns, 2 skeins each of color no. 113 and 149.

Gauge: 15 stitches = 4 inches (10 cm)

Finished size: 27 by 27 inches (69 by 69 cm)

Abbreviations:
tbl = through back of loop
wyif = with yarn in front (bring yarn to front between needles)
wyib = with yarn in back
st = stitch

Before you begin:

• Always knit the first st of the row tbl; always slip the last st of the row purlwise, wyif; always slip as if to purl.

• Each row of the graph equals two rows of mosaic knitting. Look at the graph on the right-side rows only.

• Each square of the graph equals one stitch. Shaded squares = scarlet: empty squares = silver.

• Use only one color of yarn at a time. Don't cut yarns, because you'll be able to pick them up when you're ready to use them again.

• Check the rightmost block in the row. Whatever color that block represents is the color to use for the next two rows of knitting.

• When a right-side row starts with a scarlet square, knit all the scarlet sts, and slip all the silver sts wyib. Turn. On the wrong side, knit all the scarlet sts, and slip all the silver sts wyif.

• When a right-side row starts with a silver square, knit all the silver sts, and slip all the other sts wyib. Turn. On the wrong side, knit all the silver sts, and slip all the scarlet sts wyif.

DESIGN
SUZANN THOMPSON

"A CONTENTED LIFE FOR A DOG IS A
REPETITION THAT HOLDS NO BOREDOM
OR DISAPPOINTMENT. WALK, BISCUIT,
DRINK, NAP, AND SO MANY OTHER
HAPPY RECURRENCES—THEY'RE ALL
POSITIONS ON THE FACE OF
A DOG'S NATURAL CLOCK."
—MICHAEL J. ROSEN, *DOG PEOPLE*

1

With scarlet, cast on 103 sts;
turn. K first st tbl, knit
across to last st, slip last st
wyif. This completes the
bottom row of the graph.

2

Attach silver and begin
working the graph accord-
ing to the notes above, reading right to left, the second
row from the bottom. So
you'll feel confident reading
the graph, here are written
instructions for the first silver rows: k 1st st tbl, k 1 sl
1 wyib, (k 1, sl 3 wyib) 24
times, k 1 sl 1 wyib, k 1, sl
1 wyif. Turn. K 1st st tbl,

then knit all the silver sts,
and slip all the scarlet sts
wyif, sl last st wyif.

3

Continue working the graph
this way. When you have
worked all the rows of the
graph, bind off in scarlet on
the next row. Darn in the
ends.

Canine Culture

Whoever says a mastiff can't enjoy Mozart…or a pound puppy's too uncouth for poetry…or a shitzsu won't sit still for Steinbeck obviously doesn't know a papillon from a Pekingese. Here are some recommendations for the rest of us— bedtime stories and rainy-day videos. No music. The truth is, even taking into account "Old Blue" (and, arguably, "Old Dog Tray"), the great dog song has yet to be written. The only dog songs most people know are "(How Much Is That) Doggie in the Window" and "(You Ain't Nothin' but a) Hound Dog"—lyrics I wouldn't expose a dog to.

Bedtime Stories for Pups

Big Dog, Little Dog, by P.D. Eastman

Clifford, the Small Red Puppy, by M. Bridwell

Angus and the Cat, by Marjorie Flack

Big Red, by J. Kjelgaard

Lassie Come-Home, by Eric Knight

Mush, A Dog from Space, by Daniel Pinkwater

The Dog that Stole Football Plays, by Matt Christopher

Reading for the More Mature Dog

Travels with Charlie, by John Steinbeck

Lad: A Dog, by Albert Payson Terhune

Hound of the Baskervilles, by A. Conan Doyle

Nop's Trials, by Donald McCaig

Sounder, by William Armstrong

Old Yeller, by F. Gipson

Films: Two Paws Up*

Homeward Bound

Turner and Hooch

The Fox and the Hound

The Incredible Journey

101 Dalmatians

Benji

Rin-Tin-Tin

*Warning—the following are not really dog flicks: *My Life As a Dog, Reservoir Dogs, Dog Day Afternoon.*

Autograph Hound Albums

What dog doesn't deserve it's own photo albums, journal, diary, scrapbook—the thrill of blank pages to fill with sonnets or doggerel? You can either make these books from scratch or buy blank books and decorate your heart out.

MATERIALS AND TOOLS

For the Album

A blank book or...

1 sheet of corrugated paper

10-12 sheets of good quality copy paper

Metallic embroidery thread or perle cotton

Large-eyed needle

Craft knife

Awl

Scissors

Piece of cardboard (as work area)

For Decorations

White craft glue

Scissors

Wire cutters (optional) and...

Assorted ribbons, decorative papers, cardboard, mica, small plastic frame, dog prints, canine-theme costume jewelry, metallic thread

1

To make your own book: Decide on page size—in the photo, 5" by 7" or 5-1/2" by 8-1/2" (13 by 18 cm or 14 by 22 cm). For pages, cut copy paper to size. For the cover, cut the corrugated paper with a sharp craft knife (don't press down hard or you'll crush the corrugation). Using the cardboard to protect your work surface, stack your pages between the covers; align the edges.

2

To sew the book: With the awl, make three evenly spaced holes through the stack along the right-hand edge about 1/2" (1.5 cm) from the edge. Sew from back to front, leaving a tail of thread hanging loose at the back: Starting at the center hole, sew around the spine and back up through the same hole. Sew down into the bottom hole; again wrap your thread around the spine and come back up. Bring the thread around the lower edge of the spine and sew back up the spine. When you reach the top hole, sew the top as for the bottom. End back where you began and tie off the thread.

3

Hints for decorating: Hunting canine jewelry, photos, and prints is a great excuse to go to flea markets and yard sales! To attach costume jewelry pieces, cut the pin backs off with wire cutters and attach to the book with thick, heavy craft glue; after gluing, weight the cover with a book until the glue has dried thoroughly.

"HUMANS HAVE EXTERNALIZED THEIR WISDOM—STORED IT IN MUSEUMS, LIBRARIES, THE EXPERTISE OF THE LEARNED. DOG WISDOM IS INSIDE THE BLOOD AND BONES."
—DONALD MCCAIG, *NOP'S TRIALS*

DESIGN
TERRY TAYLOR

Canny Canine Quilt

Even if you've never seen a Scottish terrier, you'll appreciate the graphic look of its profile on this small quilt—a charming canine tribute, on the wall or in a crib.

Before you begin:
All seams are 1/4" (1 cm). Fabric-cutting measurements already include seam allowance. If you want dogs facing each other, as in the photo, remember to make twelve dogs facing right and twelve facing left. These directions are for right-facing dogs; reverse them for left-facing. The quilt pictured uses a variety of fabrics for the Scotties and the backgrounds, but the materials list assumes just one dark and one light fabric for these. It's a good idea to make a test block before you cut all your fabric, that is, cut the pieces for one block and sew it as directed to make sure it works.

MATERIALS AND TOOLS

1/4 yd. (23.5 cm) of dark fabric (for dogs)

1/4 yd. (23.5 cm) of light fabric (for background)

1/3 yd. (31 cm) of fabric for inner border

1/3 yd. (31 cm) of coordinating fabric for middle border

2/3 yd. (62 cm) of dog-pattern fabric for outer border

1-1/2 yd. (1.4 m) of dog-pattern fabric for back

Batting, 40" by 60" (103 by 154 cm)

Neutral thread

Pencil

6-strand embroidery floss or #3 perle cotton (for tying)

Sewing machine (no zigzag required)

> "THERE'S FACTS ABOUT DOGS, AND THERE'S OPINIONS ABOUT THEM. THE DOGS HAVE THE FACTS, AND THE HUMANS HAVE THE OPINIONS. IF YOU WANT FACTS ABOUT A DOG, ALWAYS GET THEM STRAIGHT FROM THE DOG."
> —J. ALLEN BOONE,
> *KINSHIP WITH ALL LIFE*

Cutting

1

For each dog square: Cut, from dark fabric: seven 1-1/2" (4 cm) squares; one 3-1/2" by 2-1/2" (9 by 6.5 cm) rectangle; one 2-1/2" (6.5 cm) square. From light fabric: one 4-1/2" by 2-1/2" (11.5 by 6.5 cm) rectangle; one 2-1/2" by 1-1/2" (6.5 cm by 4 cm) rectangle; two 3-1/2" by 1-1/2" (9 by 4 cm) rectangles; one 1-1/2" (4 cm) square.

2

For inner border, cut five strips 1-1/2" by 45" (4 by 115.5 cm). For middle border, cut four strips 2-1/2" by 45" (6.5 by 115.5 cm). For outer border, cut four strips 4-1/2" by 45" (11.5 by 115.5 cm).

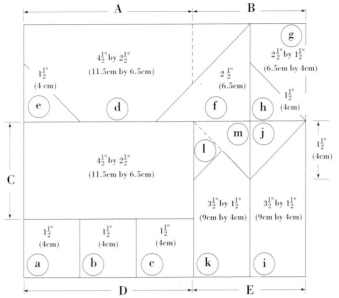

Dog Blocks

1

For the legs: sew one 1-1/2" (4 cm) square of dark fabric between two 1-1/2" (4 cm) squares of light fabric (a, b, c in drawing—refer to the drawing as you go along).

2

For the ears and tail (d, e, f in drawing), you'll need one 1-1/2" (4 cm) square and one 2-1/2" (6.5 cm) square of dark fabric and one 4-1/2" by 2-1/2" (10 by 6.5) rectangle of light fabric. On wrong side of both dark squares, pencil a diagonal line from corner to corner. On right side of light fabric, place smaller square in lower left corner and larger square

in lower right corner, right sides down. Stitch along your penciled lines. Trim to 1/4" (1 cm) the dark-fabric seam that will be covered when you fold the ear and tail into place; press the seam open.

3

For the top of the muzzle (g, h), in the same way sew one 1-1/2" (4 cm) dark square to the lower left corner of one 2-1/2" by 1-1/2" (6.5 by 4 cm) light rectangle.

4

For the muzzle bottom (i, j), in the same way sew one 1-1/2" (4 cm) dark square to the top left corner of one 3-1/2" by 1-1/2" (9 by 4 cm) light rectangle.

5

For the neck (k, l), in the same way sew one 1-1/2" (4 cm) dark square to the top right corner of one 3-1/2" by 1-1/2" (9 by 4 cm) light rectangle. Sew another 1-1/2" (4 cm) dark square (m) to the top left corner of the rectangle, crossing the first square. On right side, press open. Sew the two rectangles together, as shown (E).

6

Sew pieces A to B, C to D, then C/D to E, then C/D/E to A/B, as shown. Repeat for the other twenty-three dog blocks.

Quilt Top

1

Sew four dog blocks together; repeat until you have six large blocks, each with four dogs.

2

For the sashing (borders between blocks): Cut eight 10-1/2" (27 cm) strips from the lengths of inner-border fabric. Sew one strip to the bottom of each of the large blocks, right sides together. Then sew three of these blocks together vertically, right sides together. Finally, sew a strip of inner border fabric to the top of the upper block, right sides together. You now have joined three large blocks with borders at top and bottom and sashing between blocks. Repeat with the other three blocks.

3

For the inner border and center sashing: Cut three 33-1/2" (86 cm) strips of inner-border fabric. Pin one strip to the long left side of each rectangle of blocks, right sides together; stitch. Pin the third strip to the long right side of one rectangle, right sides together; stitch. Pin the two rectangles, right sides together, so that there is one border strip on each side and one in the middle; stitch.

4

For the borders: Pin middle border strips to top and bottom of the quilt center, right sides together; stitch. Pin middle border strips to sides, right sides together, then stitch. Repeat for the outer border.

Finishing

1

Sandwich the batting between the backing fabric and the quilt top; be sure batting and backing reach at least an inch (3 cm) beyond the top, all the way around. Pin or baste the three pieces together. (Don't stitch yet.)

2

To hand tie the quilt: Plan to tie the quilt with six strands of embroidery floss or perle cotton at about 3" (8 cm) intervals. Thread a large-eyed needle (don't knot the thread). For each tie: From the top, push the needle down through all the quilt layers and bring it back up, making a stitch of no more than 1/4" (1 cm) on the underside. Cut the floss, leaving tails long enough to tie. Tie with a double knot, then trim the ends to about 1/2"-3/4" (1.5-2 cm).

3

Trim backing and batting to match quilt top size. To bind top and bottom: Cut two strips of outer border material 2" by 35" (5 by 90 cm) and two strips 2" by 45" (5 by 115.5 cm). Fold the shorter strips in half lengthwise, wrong sides together, and press. Pin one strip to the upper edge of the quilt top, raw edges of binding and quilt edge together; stitch. Repeat at lower edge of quilt. At upper edge, fold binding to back of quilt and hand sew using any blind stitch, just covering the line of machine stitching underneath. Trim excess at ends. Repeat for lower edge.

4

To bind sides: Fold, press, and pin one longer strip to each side, as for top and bottom. Before you stitch, trim the ends to 1/2" (1.5 cm) beyond the quilt, then fold them in and under so that no raw edge will show when you fold the binding over to the back; pin. Now stitch, and continue as for top and bottom.

Care of your quilt: Machine or hand wash as for any delicate fabric; hang or lay flat to dry—don't machine dry.

DESIGN
SUSAN
DRISCOLL

82

Slip a hot-water bottle into this fuzzy cover to keep your new puppy warm or to comfort an old dog exhausted from a long day of learning new tricks.

MATERIAL AND TOOLS

1/2 yd. (46 cm) of fake fur fabric

1/4 yd. (23 cm) of white velour (or color of your choice)

Fusible web

Matching thread

12" (31 cm) of hook-and-loop tape, 1" (3 cm) wide

Sewing machine (optional)

Basic sewing equipment

Iron

Hot-water bottle

1

Enlarge the pattern on page 116 to a size slightly larger than your hot-water bottle.

2

For the front: Pin the pattern to the fake fur (black here) and cut around the edges. Referring to the photo, trace the pattern pieces for fur patches and face (white in the photo) on fusible web. Bond paper side up to the wrong side of the white velour, using a hot, dry iron. Hold up to a windowpane to draw eyes and nose features. Remove paper backing. Then bond white patches and face to the piece of black fur, using a hot, dry iron.

3

Appliqué leg, head, and ear details in light-colored thread. Appliqué eyes and nose in black thread.

4

For the back: Cut two pieces of fake fur 7" by 14" (18 by 36 cm). On the long side of each piece, turn under and sew a 1" (3 cm) hem. For the back closure, sew three squares of hook-and-loop tape evenly spaced on each back piece along the hem. Fasten the tape squares while you finish making the cover.

5

To finish the cover: Pin the front to the back, right sides together. Stitch a 1/4" (1 cm) seam, following the dog detail on the front. Trim away the excess fabric from the back. On a cold night or when your new puppy comes home, insert a warm hot-water bottle for some welcome comfort.

DESIGN NANCY ASMUS

> "HAPPINESS IS A WARM PUPPY."
> —CHARLES SCHULZ

Dogs Can Sell Anything (Except, Maybe, Cat Food)

From beer to cameras, football teams to credit cards—put a dog next to it and lots of people will rush to buy it, use it, or cheer for it.

And some breeds work better for particular products than others. Scotties may sell Scotch, but it apparently takes a real "he"-dog to sell beer. And the winner's circle hasn't featured a team in living memory whose mascot was, for instance, a cocker spaniel.

Football teams prefer English bulldogs. They look tough and strong and unbeatable. Probably the best-known bulldog in the country is Uga, the University of Georgia's mascot. Other schools with canine mascots (and teams named for dog breeds) include Yale's Bulldogs, the University of Washington Huskies, and—perhaps not as well known—the Wofford (Spartanburg, S.C.) Boston Bulls and the Titusville (Florida) High School (Boston) Terriers.

These days you can put your own dog's picture on all kinds of products—mugs, address labels, even a credit card, since the Ralston-Purina folks teamed up with a major issuer of MasterCards: You get your dog on your card plus some other goodies, Purina gets a nice data bank of dog owners, and profits from the card help support the Purina Pets for People Program, a nonprofit group that helps seniors adopt pets from animal shelters.

Meanwhile...Go Dogs!

University of Georgia mascot Uga V was born in 1990. His father, Uga IV, appeared in black tie at the 1982 Heisman Trophy banquet and also received the highest posthumous honor available to Georgia mascots, a varsity letter.

Even with your dog's photo on a Picture-Perfect Pets Purina MasterCard, you can't charge much to your dog.

84

A handsome bag for keeping toys or other dog paraphernalia—perfect for trips, too. Start with a bought canvas tote—any size, any color.

MATERIALS AND TOOLS

Canvas tote

Cardboard

Acrylic paints in desired colors

Soft-bristle artist's brush, medium

Matte medium (from a craft store)

Paint pens

"HE WAS ALWAYS SORRY, MOTHER SAID, AFTER HE BIT SOMEONE, BUT WE COULD NOT UNDERSTAND HOW SHE FIGURED THIS OUT. HE DIDN'T ACT SORRY."
—JAMES THURBER, "THE DOG THAT BIT PEOPLE"

1
To hold the canvas tight for painting and to keep paint from seeping through onto the back of the tote: Cut a piece of cardboard to fit inside the bag; tape the bag tightly onto this form.

2
Pencil a dog shape in the center and add hearts or other decorations you like. Paint these with acrylic paint straight out of the tube (you pick the color)—thinned with a little matte medium. Let dry.

3
Add border detail and any other design elements you like—spirals, dots, stars, and so on. Let dry.

4
Use paint pens to add detail.

DESIGN
KATHY COOPER

TAIL-WAGGER TIP
Make a simple toy your teething puppy will love by tying a firm knot in an old cotton terry towel. Fit the size to the dog—older dogs enjoy these too. Great fun to shake, carry around, or just chew on.

Let-Sleeping-Dogs-Lie Bed

The beauty of this bed lies in its age, style, and recycled character—you make it from an old chair you scout out at a used-furniture store or yard sale. The instructions apply to any ladder-back chair with arms, and since your chair will be unique, consider the measurements approximate... and trust your judgment.

MATERIALS

Old chair with arms

2 rough-sawn planks, 10" by 38" (26 by 97.5 cm)

Pine scrap, 1" by 2" by 5" (3 by 5 by 13 cm) (optional—for bone)

3/4" (2 cm) plywood, 18" by 36" (46 by 92.5 cm)

4 wood balls, 1-1/4" diameter (3.5 cm)

4 dowels, 3/8" by 2" (1.25 by 5 cm)

Trim: 2 1" by 18" (3 by 46 cm) and 2 1" by 34-1/2" (3 by 88.5 cm) (for plywood supports)

Assorted screws

Glue

Stain

TOOLS

Screwdriver

Drill with 3/8" and 1/8" bits (1.25 and .5 cm)

Jigsaw

1

Take apart the old chair. The back will be the headboard. The front legs and chair rails will be the footboard. Save all the other parts!

2

Fasten the planks (the side rails of the bed) to the chair back (the headboard), with the top edge of the plank even with the spot where the top of the seat once attached—about 13" (33.5 cm) off the ground. Pre-drill holes in the planks using 1/8" (.5 cm) drill bit, then secure with several screws.

3

As trim, attach the chair arms, armrests facing out, to the top of the side rails and to the headboard.

4

Mount the planks (side rails) to the footboard using the jigsaw to notch the planks as necessary to fit around the original chair rails (if any). Drill and screw to secure.

5

For the plywood supports: Drill and screw the short lengths of trim to the inside of the headboard and footboard about 4-1/2" (11.5 cm) below the top of the side rails. Attach the long trim to the side rails about 4-1/2" (11.5 cm) from the top. This assembly will support the plywood on which the mattress (a pillow) will rest.

6

Use any remaining chair parts as fillers or decoration as you like. Drill 3/8" (1.25 cm) holes 1/2" (1.5 cm) deep in the balls and the top of each corner post. Put a small amount of glue in each hole, then insert one end of the dowels in the balls and glue the other ends into the posts.

7

Stain all surfaces of the bed, including the plywood. If you choose to, carve a bone out of the small piece of pine and drill and screw it to the top of the headboard.

> "THERE ARE NO ONE-NIGHT STANDS WITH A DOG. ONCE YOU LET YOUR PET INTO YOUR BED, IT'S HARD TO GET HIM OUT."
> —DIANA DELMAR,
> *THE GUILT-FREE DOG OWNER'S GUIDE*

DESIGN
ROLF
HOLMQUIST

TAIL - WAGGER TIP

Your dog wants to sleep as close to you as possible because in many ways it's still a puppy and you're its surrogate "mother" (and also of course because it loves you very much). Among wolves, only pack out-casts sleep away from the group—so if you have only one dog, it may feel shunned at bedtime if it can't sleep, if not with you, at least nearby.

Let-Sleeping-Dogs-Lie Tied Quilt, Mattress, and Pillow

The pièce de resistance for the Let-Sleeping-Dogs-Lie Bed. The directions for this quilt allow you to adjust its size easily to make a soft lie-upon for bigger dogs.

MATERIALS AND TOOLS

2 yds. of dog-print fabric

1 yd. of coordinating solid-color fabric

1 yd. of backing fabric (for quilt)

1 yd. of polyester batting

1 large bag of polyester fiberfill

1 skein of rug yarn in complementary color

Matching thread

Sewing machine

Basic sewing equipment

"LET SLEEPING DOGS LIE— WHO WANTS TO ROUSE EM?"
—CHARLES DICKENS, DAVID COPPERFIELD

Mattress and Pillow

1

All seams are 1/4" (1 cm). Measure the inside of the dog bed and add 1/4" (1 cm) on each side for seams; cut two pieces of dog-print fabric to this measurement. Machine sew the two pieces together, right sides together, leaving a 4" (10 cm) opening. Turn right side out, fill with fiberfill, and hand sew the opening closed.

2

Make the pillow using the same directions, to the size you want.

Quilt

1

Measure the length of the bed, then the width plus the amount of overlap you want your quilt to have. Divide the length and width each by 3-1/4" (8.5 cm); multiply these two numbers to find out the number of 3-1/4" (8.5 cm) squares you need for the quilt. Cut half this number from the dog print, half from the solid print.

2

Machine sew squares together (right sides together) to make lengthwise strips that equal your measured quilt length, alternating fabrics—be sure to start each strip with alternating fabric squares. When you have enough strips to equal your measured quilt width, sew them together, right sides together.

3

Cut batting and backing to your quilt measurements. Baste the batting to the wrong side of the backing. Then pin the backing to your patched piece, right sides together. Sew around all four sides, leaving a 6" (15 cm) opening. Turn right side out and hand sew the opening closed.

4

To hand tie the quilt: Plan to tie the quilt at the corners of the squares. Thread a large-eyed needle with rug yarn (don't knot the thread). For each tie: From the patched side, push the needle through all the quilt layers and bring it back up, making a stitch of no more than 1/4" (1 cm) on the underside. Cut the yarn, leaving tails long enough to tie. Tie with a double knot, then trim the ends to about 1/2"-3/4" (1.5-2 cm).

DESIGN
DIANE HOLMQUIST

Dog Star Photo Frame

A colorful frame for the bright Spot in your life, this project is as easy to do as it looks. Your handwriting—or your child's—makes it unique…and instead of breeds (or along with them) you might choose to record the names of all the dogs in your family's history.

MATERIALS AND TOOLS

Unfinished frame (with glass and backing)

Sandpaper

Acrylic paint

Permanent fine-line gold marking pen

Acrylic sealer (optional)

"DOG. A KIND OF ADDITIONAL OR SUBSIDIARY DEITY DESIGNED TO CATCH THE OVERFLOW AND SURPLUS OF THE WORLD'S WORSHIP."
—AMBROSE BIERCE

1

Sand the unfinished frame to remove surface blemishes. Pay special attention to the joins.

2

Prepare the frame surface either with paint or acrylic sealer; allow to dry.

3

Give the frame two or three coats of paint, allowing it to dry thoroughly between coats.

4

Write the names of dog breeds or other dog lore on the face and sides of the frame. (You can get breed names from an encyclopedia.) Try out your style on the back, if you like. Rotate the frame as you go, so the words won't all face the same direction. Ink in dots or other decorative accents in the spaces, if you choose.

DESIGN
TERRY TAYLOR

Dog-Days Nap Cushion

Something about this bed makes it irresistible not only to canines but to cats, too. It's one of the simplest sewing projects in the book—guaranteed to be in frequent use not just during summer's dog days but year round.

MATERIALS AND TOOLS

2-2/3 yd. (2.4 m) of washable fabric

2 yd. (1.8 m) of upholstery batting

Matching or neutral thread

Sewing machine

Basic sewing equipment

Iron

1

Wash fabric before measuring, as it may shrink; press if necessary. Cut fabric to 96" by 32" (247 by 82 cm). On each end, fold over and pin a 5" (13 cm) hem on wrong side.

2

Lay piece flat, right side up. Measure in 25" (64 cm) from each fold; fold the left-hand 25" (64 cm) segment toward the center, then the right-hand segment, which will overlap the left by about 15" (38.5 cm). Pin along top and bottom, and sew with a 3/8" (1.25 cm) seam allowance, removing pins as you sew.

3

Turn piece right side out and place batting inside.

> "I SOMETIMES LOOK INTO THE FACE OF MY DOG STAN AND SEE WISTFUL SADNESS AND EXISTENTIAL ANGST WHEN ALL HE IS ACTUALLY DOING IS SLOWLY SCANNING THE CEILING FOR FLIES."
> —MERRILL MARKOE,
> *WHAT THE DOGS HAVE TAUGHT ME*

DESIGN
SUSAN DRISCOLL

91

"These Are Mine" Toy Box or
Stretch Limo Travel Box / Booster Seat

Dress this handy box up or down, depending on your dog's taste. If you use it as a booster seat, link a seatbelt through the handles to hold it in place—and for your dog's safety, you might think about using a harness (available from pet stores or dog magazines). For a lighter-weight box, use plywood instead of pine.

MATERIALS

1" by 12" (2.5 by 31 cm) pine, 10' (3.1 m): cut 4 20" (51 cm) lengths (for the top, bottom, front, and back);2 17-1/8" (44 cm) lengths (for the ends)

2 1-1/2" by 1-1/2" (4 by 4 cm) brass hinges

1-1/2" (4 cm) nails

1-1/2" (4 cm) wood screws

3/8" (1.25 cm) dowel, 6" (15 cm)

Wood filler

Glue

TOOLS

Drill with 3/8" (1.25 cm) and 1" (3 cm) bits

Jigsaw

Compass

Handsaw

Router with 1/4" (1 cm) roundover bit

Wood chisel

Sandpaper (fine)

"**I WOULD RATHER TRAIN A STRIPED ZEBRA TO BALANCE AN INDIAN CLUB THAN INDUCE A DACHSHUND TO HEED MY SLIGHTEST COMMAND.**"
—E. B. WHITE, "DOG TRAINING"

MATERIALS AND TOOLS FOR PAINTING

Oil-based enamel paints (here, blue, yellow, and white)

Painter's masking tape

Sponge applicator, rag, or sponge

Alphabet stencil

Small paintbrush or stenciling brush

Pencil

DESIGN
MIKE HESTER

1

For the bottom: Cut one of the long pieces of 1" by 12" (2.5 by 31 cm) to a width of 9-5/8" (24.75 cm).

2

For the back: On another long piece, measure in 3-1/2" (9 cm) from each end, and trace the hinge on the edge so the knuckle overhangs the back. With the wood chisel, cut an indentation at each tracing deep enough to allow the closed hinge to lie flush.

3

For the ends: On each of the two shorter pieces, draw the top curve using the compass set at half the width of the board.

4

For the bone handles: On the end pieces, measure 3-1/2" (9 cm) in from each side and lightly draw a line parallel to the side. On each line, mark down from the top 1-3/4" and 2-3/4" (4.5 and 7 cm). Drill 1" (3 cm) holes at these four points. Connect these holes by lightly drawing two lines parallel to the top edge at 1-7/8" and 2-5/8" (4.75 and 6.75 cm). Cut these lines and the top curve with the jigsaw. Use the router to roundover the dog bone inside and out.

5

To put the box together: Nail the bottom to the front and back pieces along the lower edge (the bottom is recessed). On each end piece, mark three points spaced evenly up each side and one centered along the lower edge. Drill a 3/8" (1.25 cm) hole about a third of the thickness of the board deep at these points. Use screws in the holes to attach the ends to the front, back, and bottom.

6

To hinge and finish: On the back, mount the hinges in the recesses you cut and then screw the hinges to the top, making sure the top lies flat and square. To fill the screw holes, put a dab of glue on the end of the dowel and insert it in a screw hole on the end, tap it snug, then cut it flush with the hand saw. Repeat this with all the screw holes. Fill the nail holes along the front and back edges with wood filler. Sand smooth all surfaces.

7

Make pastel blue and yellow paint by mixing each paint with white. With masking tape, mark off the areas you don't want to rub the first color of paint on. Then rub the paint on evenly with your applicator or rag and keep rubbing until you get an effect you like—more or less grain showing through. Repeat with the second color of paint.

8

When the paint is completely dry, decorate with the dog pattern on page 112 or any pattern you like. Stencil your dog's name on the box wherever you want to, and as many times as your dog will appreciate. When all paint is dry, finish with matte polyurethane or another protective finish.

Art Deco Memorial

A handsome contemporary marker to place as a memorial to your dog or to mark your dog's grave is something worth spending special thought and time on. The inscription on this marker is wood burned, but you might prefer to hand letter your message with paint.

MATERIALS

- *2" by 11-1/4" (5 by 29 cm) cedar or redwood, 30" (77 cm)*
- *1-1/4" (3.5 cm) galvanized finish nails*
- *Sandpaper (medium and fine)*

TOOLS

- *Yardstick or straight edge*
- *Compass*
- *Jigsaw (or band saw, etc.)*
- *Hammer*
- *File, plane, or router with chamfer bit (to round edges)*

1

At one end of the board, mark 1-1/4" (3.5 cm) and 2-1/2" (6.5 cm) from each edge. This will be the top of the memorial. On the opposite end, mark 1" (3 cm) and 1-1/2" (4 cm) from each edge. This will be the bottom. Using a yardstick, draw lines connecting the top and bottom inner marks, then the outer marks.

2

To draw the curves: Draw a line down the center of the board from top to bottom. Measure down 5" (13 cm) and mark, 6-3/4" (17.5 cm) and mark, 10" (26 cm) and mark. With the compass set at a 5" (13 cm) radius, set the compass point on the highest mark and draw the top curve; on the middle mark and draw the first side curve; on the bottom mark and draw the outer curve.

3

With the jigsaw, carefully cut along the vertical outer lines to separate the four pieces, then cut the top curves on each section. Shorten the two inner sections to 25-1/2" (65.5 cm) and the outer sections to 20-3/4" (53 cm), tapering the bottoms. *Use a firm straight edge as a guide for your jigsaw when cutting the tapered lines.*

4

Use a plane, file, or router to round or chamfer the front edges of all pieces. Sand all surfaces with medium, then fine, sandpaper.

5

Nail the sections back in their original pattern—or rearrange them into a design that pleases you more. The finish nails here are spaced 1-1/4" (3.5 cm) and 3/4" (2 cm) from each top edge.

6

Wood burn or paint an epitaph, if you like, then finish with a waterproof sealer, which will protect the paint and preserve the natural wood color. (Without the seal, the marker will weather to a soft gray.)

> "YOU THINK DOGS WILL NOT BE IN HEAVEN? I TELL YOU, THEY WILL BE THERE LONG BEFORE ANY OF US."
> —ROBERT LOUIS STEVENSON

DESIGN
MARK STROM

Dear
TROIKA

1971-1985

*Forever
in our
Hearts*

*Dick and Margaret Kralin's companion, Troika, a Hungarian puli, was a devoted
mother, a faithful friend, and a dog of incredible principle and compassion .*

A memorial marker designed by Mark Strom for Lee, my beloved golden retriever,
who all of her life did her running with only three paws.

All Dogs Go to Heaven

We're funny about our dogs. Some (but not I) might say obsessed (but not all of us). For instance, all dogs certainly go to heaven, but what happens when they leave *here* and exactly how they get *there* depends a lot on their owners—just like their lives on earth did.

You may not know it, but a whole industry exists to meet the needs of people whose pets have died. Not just grief counselors and pet cemeteries, but headstones and caskets, photo urns, crematories, grief newsletters, cemeteries with chapels and viewing rooms, and—one of the most recent twists—cryogenic freezing and storage of a pet's blood for possible cloning, maybe in as few as ten years.

Like most such services, the St. Francis Pet Crematory in Greenville, South Carolina, will deliver a pet's ashes (known in the business as "cremains") in a wood box for burial or in a container of the owner's choice. One entrepreneur offers to blend these ashes with slurry and handcraft a ceramic model of the pet, as a memorial.

A company on the west coast of Florida reportedly will fly a pet's ashes over the Gulf of Mexico in a polyester-film balloon, which eventually bursts from heat or atmospheric pressure, scattering the contents over the water.

Letting go of someone entirely loveable and undemanding who has loved you unconditionally isn't easy. That's probably why freezing their pet's DNA appeals to some people. As the developer of Geneti Pet said, "Your pet is gone, in a sense, but not really...If we don't save their DNA now, no amount of money will be able to bring them back...If scientists are in fact able to create higher life forms through genetic engineering, then we're ready."

Apparently these people haven't read Stephen King's *Pet Cemetery*. Call me a scaredy cat, but I think sometimes it's best not to fool with either Father Time or Mother Nature.

The entrance to the cemetery of the Greenville, S.C., Humane Society.

The Memory Garden wall in the Henderson County, N.C., Humane Society's Petland Memorial Cemetery.

Little Old Dog Sampler

Even Edith Wharton, that chronicler of upper-class manners, had a sentimental streak when it came to her dog. (You can work this sampler in its most basic form by leaving out the inner "bones" border and simply backstitching the dog, ball, and dish.)

MATERIALS AND TOOLS

14-count evenweave fabric, 12" by 14" (31 by 36 cm) or 18-count evenweave fabric, 11" by 13" (28 by 33.5 cm)

DMC embroidery floss or equivalent (see chart for colors—or pick your own)

Tapestry needle

Hoop (optional)

Frame

DESIGN MEASUREMENTS:

85 by 115 stitches

14-count fabric, about 6" by 8" (15 by 21 cm); 18-count fabric, about 5" by 6-1/4" (13 by 16 cm)

DESIGN
GARNETTE
SPRINKLE

KEY TO CHART

v = 932	
z = white	
x = 931	
= = 355	
I = 642	
o = 930	
· = 645	

Backstitch:

310: Dog, dog collar,
     dog dish

930: Name

355: Mouth, ball,
     "DOG" on dish

640: Bones

1

Find the center of your fabric, then center your design
on this point, counting
threads to one edge (one
square on the chart = one
thread) to establish your
starting point.

2

Use two strands of floss for
both cross-stitching and backstitching. You might want to
put your dog's name on the
dish instead of "Dog." You
also may prefer to mat your
sampler before framing it.

Herbal Pooch Powder and
St. Bernard First-Aid Salve

Herbal Powder

Dust this aromatic, all-natural powder on your dog's bedding daily during flea season to repel fleas and ticks—and dust it directly on your dog's coat to discourage fleas and act as a deodorizer anytime. (You'll find the oils, flowers, and herbs at a health-food store.)

INGREDIENTS

1 box corn starch

1 small box baking soda

1/4 cup each of lavender flowers, pennyroyal, and yarrow

1 dropper each of cedarwood oil, lavender oil, and citronella oil

1

Mix the first two ingredients in the bowl.

2

Blend flowers and herbs until powdered and add to the bowl. Add the oils and mix well to blend.

3

Spoon carefully into containers (for instance, recycled spice jars with shaker tops) and add your own label.

TAIL-WAGGER TIP

Your dog can't catch your cold, and you can't catch your dog's cold. Different cold germs. (Etiquette still requires both of you to cover your noses when you sneeze.)

"THEY SAY A REASONABLE NUMBER OF FLEAS IS GOOD FOR A DOG—KEEPS HIM FROM BROODIN' OVER BEIN' A DOG."
—E. N. WESTCOTT, *DAVID HARUM*

RECIPES
DEBBIE MIDKIFF

Salve

A topical, all-natural herbal salve to treat flea or tick bites, cuts, scrapes, hot spots, and dry-skin irritations.

INGREDIENTS

1 tablespoon olive oil

1 tablespoon almond oil

1/2 teaspoon beeswax

1 Vitamin E capsule

10 drops camphor oil

7 drops thyme oil

7 drops tea tree oil

Before you begin:
For containers, use two recycled lip-balm containers or small pots with tops—1-ounce recycled jelly jars or cosmetic jars work well.

1

In a double boiler (or make a double boiler by placing a small bowl in a pan of water), heat the olive oil, almond oil, and beeswax over medium heat.

2

When the mixture melts, remove from heat, add the remaining ingredients and whisk until the mixture begins to thicken.

3

Pour into container. Allow to cool. Cover and add your own label.

TAIL-WAGGER TIP

The dog days, those sultry, slow-moving days from July 3 to August 11, derive their name not from days so hot that dogs go mad but from Sirius, the Dog Star. In Roman times, it was believed that the heat from the bright star in Canis Major (the Great Dog, a southern constellation that lies between Puppis and Orion) combined with the sun's heat to create the period's high temperatures. Romans called this time of high summer *dies caniculares*, days of the dog.

"WHO LOVES ME WILL LOVE MY DOG AS WELL."
—ST. BERNARD, "SERMO PRIMUS"

Bone-Garden Sign

This sign reflects a delightful and peaceful scene that you can caption however you wish and in the language of your choice—"Dog Crossing," "Cave Canem" ("Beware the Dog"), "Jardin du Chien"…you get the idea.

MATERIALS

*Outdoor-grade 1/2"
  (1.5 cm) plywood,
  15-1/2" by 9-3/4"
  (39 by 25 cm)*

White exterior paint

Acrylic paints

*Outdoor-grade
  polyurethane sealer*

Carbon paper

Pencil

TOOLS

Paintbrushes

*Sandpaper
  (medium and fine)*

Saw

DESIGN
DOLLY LUTZ MORRIS

1

Sand plywood and apply a base coat of white paint. Transfer the design from page 113 to the plywood with carbon paper and pencil.

2

Paint the sky. grass. and border areas with acrylics. Let dry. Redraw any details you've painted over using the pattern and carbon paper. Paint the details and let dry.

3

Paint with two or three coats of the sealer. per manufacturer's instructions. Let dry completely.

4

Mount on wooden stakes. hang from a chain. or attach to your dog's house.

"DOG PEOPLE ARE FOLKS WHO WANT THEIR LIVES TO BE A LITTLE DOGGIER—MORE PHYSICAL CONTACT, CONSISTENCY, INNOCENCE, WILDNESS, ROUTINE, UNSELFCONSCIOUSNESS, AND EVEN HUMILITY."
—MICHAEL J. ROSEN,
DOG PEOPLE

Boston Bull Circus Clown

A wonderful project to do with kids—create a whole circus family of dog clowns. If you can't get your dog to pose, use a photo. With the simplest of tools and equipment, voila! you're a sculptor.

MATERIALS AND TOOLS

2 polystyrene foam balls, 1" and 3" (3 and 8 cm)

Cardboard (for hat)

Instant paper-mache mix

Acrylic paints in desired colors

Clear nail polish

White glue (or hot glue and glue gun)

Matte spray sealer

Glitter paint

Manicure set or sculpting tools

Paint brushes

DESIGN
DOLLY LUTZ
MORRIS

104

1

For your armature, glue the small foam ball to the larger one. Mix the paper mache according to package instructions. (The more attention you pay to blending the mix and smoothing it carefully on the balls, the better your dog will look.) Cover the balls with a 1/2" (1.5 cm) layer of paper mache—smooth with tools and your fingers.

2

To shape the face: Add paper mache to broaden the forehead; indent the eyes with tools. Add mache for the ear, then build up the muzzle and nose area, blending and smoothing with tools. Use tools to form the mouth.

3

For the hat: Add a cardboard cone about 1-1/2" (4 cm) in diameter and 2" (5 cm) tall, and cover with a 1/4" (1 cm) layer of mache. Smooth and blend into head, adding more mache where needed.

4

Use tools to form a collar about 1-1/4" (3.5 cm) wide and create a scalloped effect; blend well into neck and body. Form front legs with a coil of mache 1-1/4" by 5/8" (3.5 by 1.75 cm); blend well into body with tools, indenting for toes.

5

Allow to dry completely. Paint with acrylics, and allow to dry thoroughly. Spray with matte sealer. Paint collar and hat with one coat of glitter paint. Paint eyes with two coats of clear nail polish to make them shine. Print up circus tickets.

"THE GREATEST PLEASURE OF A DOG IS THAT YOU MAY MAKE A FOOL OF YOURSELF WITH HIM, AND NOT ONLY WILL HE NOT SCOLD YOU, BUT HE WILL MAKE A FOOL OF HIMSELF, TOO."
—SAMUEL BUTLER

Welcome-Home Puppy Cushion

Not only is this comforting cushion covered in warm flannel, but it has a pocket in it where you can tuck a loudly ticking watch or small clock—a rhythm your new puppy may associate with the familiar sound of its mother's heart.

MATERIALS AND TOOLS

1/4 yd. (23 cm) each of 5 patterns of flannel, 36" (.9 m) wide

2/3 yd. (62 cm) of flannel, 36" (.9 m) wide (for back)

Matching thread

6" (15 cm) cm) of hook-and-loop tape, 1" (3 cm) wide

Standard bed pillow, 20" by 24" (51 by 61 cm)

Diaper pad or other water-proofing fabric, 20" by 24" (51 by 62 cm)

Sewing machine (optional)

Iron

Basic sewing equipment

DESIGN
NANCY ASMUS

1

All seams are 5/8" (1.75 cm). For the cushion cover front: Based on your five flannel patterns, plan your design of twenty flannel squares on paper (or use this design); then cut out 20 squares and lay them out according to your design. Nancy Asmus used: #1 flannel, 3 squares; #2, 5 squares; #3, #4, and #5, 4 squares each.

2

With right sides together, machine or hand stitch the five squares in the top row into one long strip. On the wrong side, press seams flat. Repeat for the next three rows. In the same way, sew the four strips together to form a rectangle of twenty squares, one side of the cushion cover.

3

For the pocket: Cut out two more 6" (15 cm) squares (in this design, flannel #5); place one on top of the other, right sides together, and machine or hand stitch three sides. Turn right side out and press flat. Turn under a small seam on the fourth side and stitch closed. Machine or hand stitch the pocket to a matching square on the cushion cover front.

4

For the back: Fold the large piece of flannel selvage edges together; cut two pieces 23" by 16" (59 by 41 cm). Serge or overcast the raw edges, then make a 2" (5 cm) hem on the shorter side of each piece.

5

For the back closure: On one back piece, sew three hook-and-loop squares evenly spaced along the hemmed area on the right side. On the other piece, on the wrong side of the hemmed area, sew three hook-and-loop squares to correspond to the first piece. Fasten the pieces together with the tape while you finish making the cover.

6

Pin the front to the back, right sides together, then sew around all four edges. To make box corners, sew across each corner as if you were making the cross piece on a capital-letter A. Turn the cover right side out.

7

To ready the cushion for your new puppy, safety pin the diaper pad to one side of the bed pillow, insert the pillow in the cover, and insert a ticking watch or clock in the pocket.

> "WHEN A PUPPY TAKES FIFTY CATNAPS IN THE COURSE OF THE DAY, HE CANNOT ALWAYS BE EXPECTED TO SLEEP THE NIGHT THROUGH. IT IS TOO MUCH TO ASK."
> —ALBERT PAYSON TERHUNE, *"THE COMING OF LAD"*

1	3	2	4	2
2	4	5	3	5
3	5*	1	4	2
4	2	3	5	1

Yuppy Puppy House

Not for yuppy puppies only, but pretty doggone upscale. And the only special tool you need is a jigsaw. (If you don't have one, get a helpful friend to do those parts for you—or better yet, show you how to use one.)

MATERIALS

5/8" (1.75 cm) exterior plywood, 4' by 8' (1.24 by 2.48 m)

1" by 4" (3 by 10 cm) pine, 2 8' lengths (2.48 m)

1" (3 cm) and 1-1/4" (3.5 cm) galvanized finish nails

Sandpaper (fine)

Caulking

Paint in the colors of your choice (exterior paint for outdoor houses)

Silicone sealant (optional)

TOOLS

Tape measure

Compass

Jigsaw

Hammer

Paintbrush

Cut List:

From plywood:

2 16" by 20"
   (41 by 51 cm)
   (front and back)

2 13" by 26"
   (33.5 by 67 cm)
   (sides)

1 18-3/4" by 26"
   (48 by 67 cm)
   (bottom)

2 13" by 33-1/4"
   (33.5 by 85.5 cm)
   (roof)

1 11-1/2" by 11-3/4"
   (29.5 by 30 cm)
   (door molding)

From 1" by 4"
(3 by 10 cm):

Front Trim

2 4-7/8" by 2-3/8"
   (12.75 by 6.25 cm)

2 4-7/8" by 1"
   (12.75 by 3 cm)

2 6-1/2" by 1"
   (17 by 3 cm)

1 21-1/2" by 1-3/4"
   (55 by 4.5 cm)

Side Trim

2 26" by 2-3/8"
   (67 by 6.25 cm)

4 26" by 1"
   (67 by 3 cm)

2 26" by 1-3/4"
   (67 by 4.5 cm)

Back Trim

1 21-1/2" by 2-3/8"
   (55 by 6.25 cm)

2 21-1/2" by 1"
   (55 by 3 cm)

1 21-1/2" by 1-3/4"
   (55 by 4.5 cm)

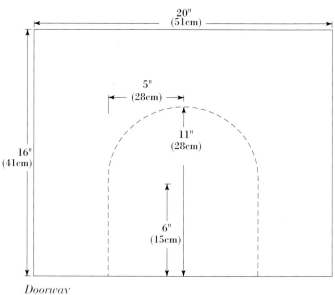

Doorway

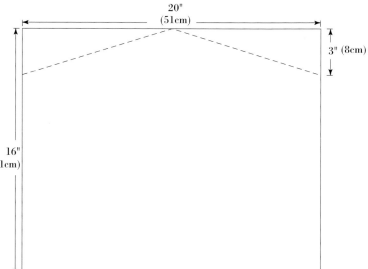

Roof Lines

DESIGN
MARK STROM

1

For the doorway: On the front piece, mark the center of both 20" (51 cm) sides and draw a line down the center of the board (see drawing). At top and bottom, measure over 5" (13 cm) on each side of the center line and mark, then draw lines joining these marks—you now have three parallel lines running down the board. From the bottom, measure up 6" and 11" (15 and 28 cm) on the center line and mark both points. Set your compass at a 5"

(13 cm) radius; set the point on the 6" (15 cm) mark. Draw an arc that intersects the 11" (28 cm) mark and the lines drawn on each side of the center line. This is the doorway.

2

For the roof lines: On both outside edges of the front piece, measure down 3" (8 cm) from the top and mark (see drawing). Draw a line from the center top (the peak of the roof) to each of these marks. This is your cutting line for the roof. Cut

"THE FIDELITY OF A DOG IS A PRECIOUS GIFT DEMANDING NO LESS BINDING MORAL RESPONSIBILITIES THAN THE FRIENDSHIP OF A HUMAN BEING. THE BOND WITH A TRUE DOG IS AS LASTING AS THE TIES OF THIS EARTH CAN EVER BE."
—KONRAD LORENZ,
MAN MEETS DOG

with the jigsaw. Repeat this step with the other 16" by 20" (41 by 51 cm) piece, for the back.

3

To make the door molding: Trace the door shape onto the door molding piece. Then draw a second line 3/4" (2 cm) outside your tracing line, all the way around. Cut out this 3/4" (2 cm) arc—it's your door molding.

4

To attach the sides and bottom of the house: Nail 1-1/4" (3.5 cm) nails through the front and back pieces into the ends of the side pieces. Insert the bottom and nail it in place with 1-1/4" (3.5 cm) nails.

5

For the roof: So the two roof pieces can fit together snugly, you'll need to use a jigsaw to angle the two edges that will join at the top. Angle the base of the jigsaw to 15° and cut along one long edge of each roof piece.

6

This is the ideal time to paint all parts of the house, including the trim. You can touch it up if you need to after it's nailed together.

7

Raising the roof: Position the roof halves on the house with equal overhang on all sides. Secure one piece to the front and back with 1-1/4" (3.5 cm) nails.

Run a bead of caulking along the peak edge, then push the other roof piece into position and secure it with nails. As an added precaution against leaks, you may want to seal the seam at the center of the roof with silicone sealant.

8

To attach the three lines of trim to the back and sides: Using 1" (3 cm) nails, attach the 1-3/4" (4.5 cm) trim snugly under the roof edge on each side of the house, then to the back. In the same way, attach the 1" (3 cm) middle trim 3/4" (2 cm) below the top trim, and the 2-3/8" (6.25 cm) bottom trim 3/4" (2 cm) below that.

9

To attach the three lines of front trim: Lay the front trim in position; then lay the door molding in place on top of the trim. Mark the curves on the trim. Cut the curves with the jigsaw. Nail the front trim in place, matching the placement of the side trim.

10

Sand all rough ends. Touch up any paint as needed.

TAIL-WAGGER TIP

People with dogs (or cats) live longer on average than those without pets. Patting a dog reduces stress and has a generally calming influence, lowering blood pressure and thus reducing the risk of heart attack. (As if we needed a more concrete reason for keeping a dog.)

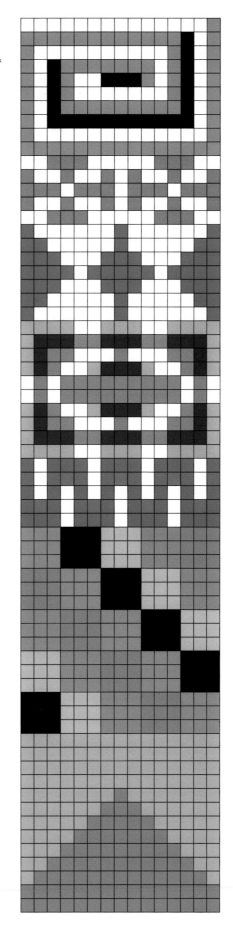

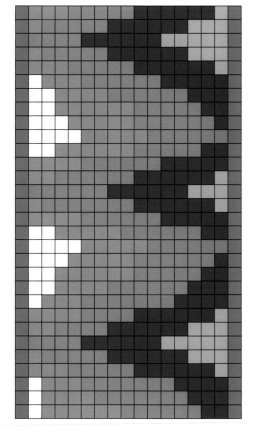

Patterns
and
Illustrations

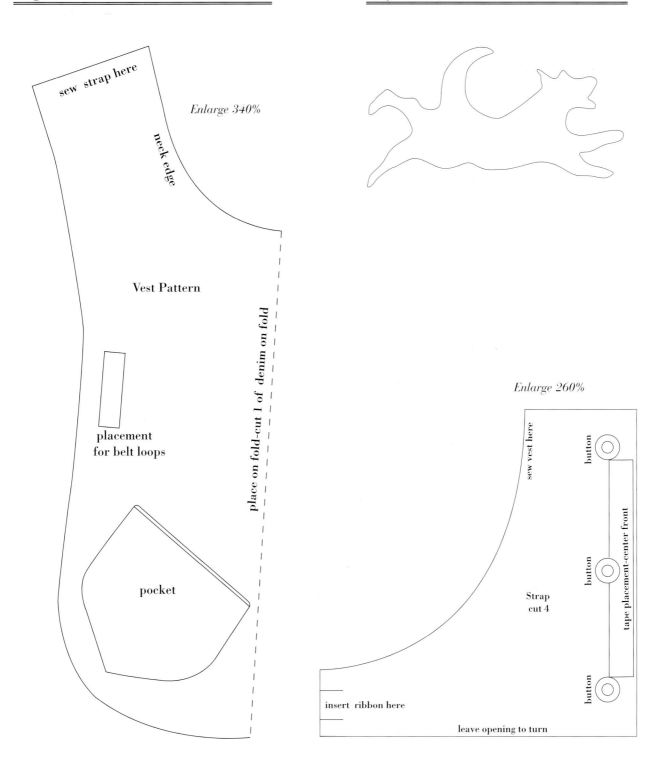

sew strap here

Enlarge 340%

neck edge

Vest Pattern

place on fold-cut 1 of denim on fold

placement
for belt loops

pocket

Enlarge 260%

sew vest here

button

tape placement-center front

button

Strap
cut 4

button

insert ribbon here

leave opening to turn

Bone Garden Sign

Leader-of-the-Pack Tux Front

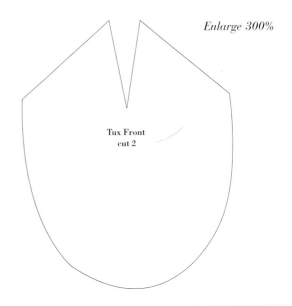

Enlarge 300%

Tux Front
cut 2

Pooch Pack

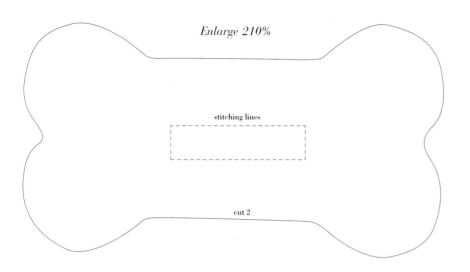

Enlarge 210%

stitching lines

cut 2

Howliday Collar Stick-Ons

Sundog Lifeguard
Emblems

Large Salty Dog Sailor Hat

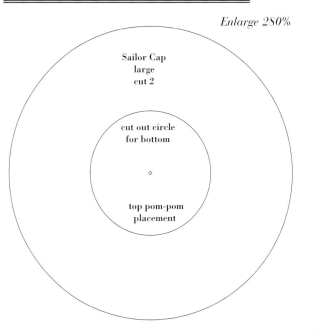

Enlarge 280%

Sailor Cap
large
cut 2

cut out circle
for bottom

top pom-pom
placement

Small Salty Dog Sailor Hat

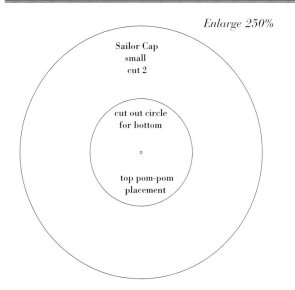

Enlarge 250%

Sailor Cap
small
cut 2

cut out circle
for bottom

top pom-pom
placement

Small Salty Dog Middy Collar

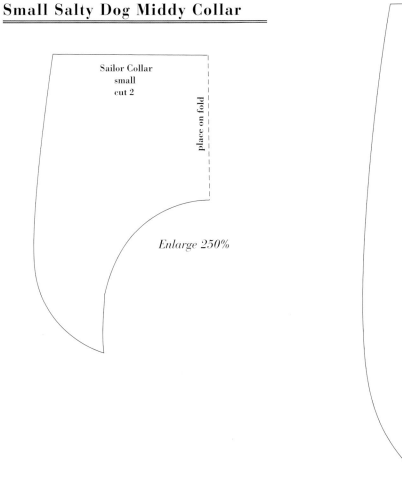

Sailor Collar
small
cut 2

place on fold

Enlarge 250%

Large Salty Dog Middy Collar

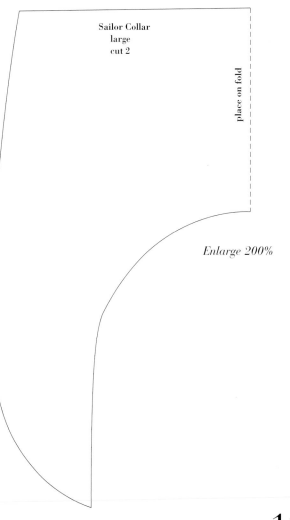

Sailor Collar
large
cut 2

place on fold

Enlarge 200%

Enlarge 200%

Enlarge 200%

BONE

APPETIT

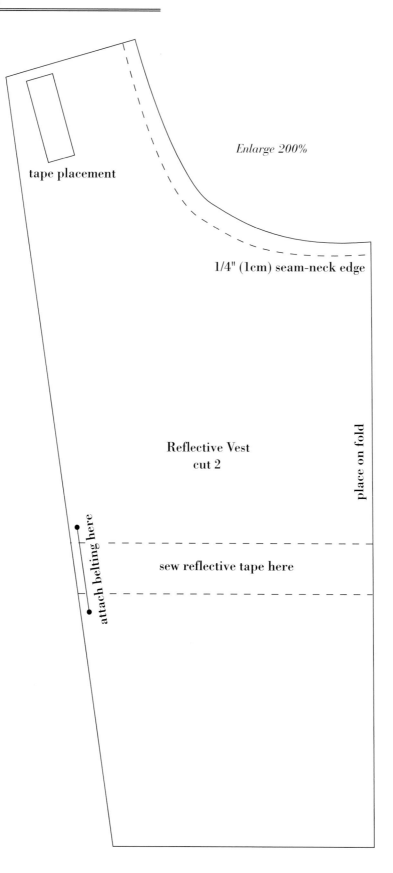

tape placement

Enlarge 200%

1/4" (1cm) seam-neck edge

place on fold

Reflective Vest
cut 2

attach belting here

sew reflective tape here

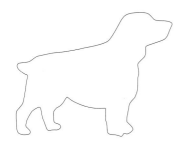

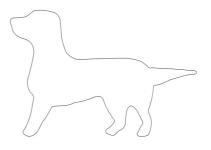

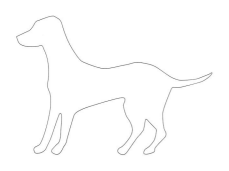

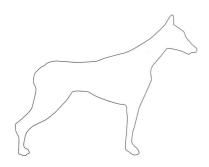

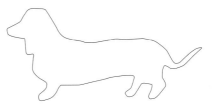

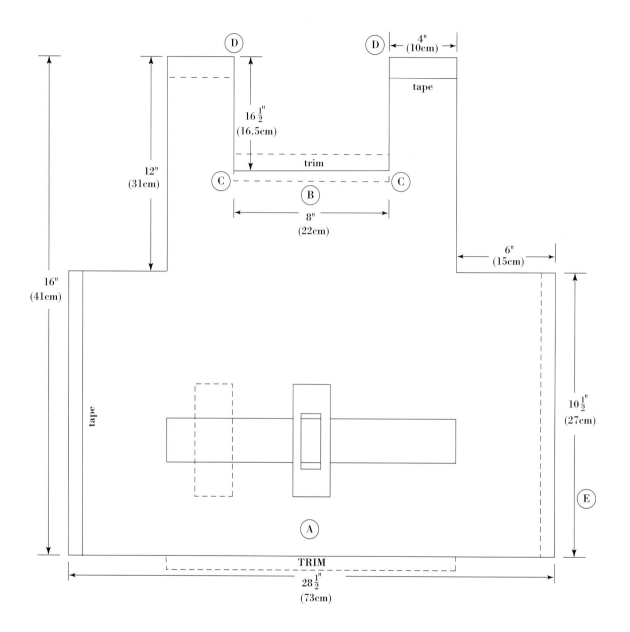

Contributing Designers

Nancy Asmus, of Conneaut Lake, Pennsylvania, is an award-winning sewer and plans to market some of her dog-theme patterns.

Maya Contento is a food stylist and gourmet cook who writes beautiful poetry and lives with three dogs, including the dachshund and Old English sheepdog in this book and Inka, a Benji-shepherd mix.

The author of the forthcoming *Complete Book of Floorcloths* (Lark, 1997), **Kathy Cooper** has loving memories of Jasmine, a golden retriever and "our first child" and now shares her home with a dalmatian, Juni Moon.

Holly Decker used to be a professional seamstress and now sews for fun; she lives with Jade, a German shepherd mix (this book's Santa Paws), who herds Holly's two sixteen-year-old cats like sheep.

Susan Driscoll quilts and gardens in Asheville, North Carolina, where she lives with two cats and no dogs, but she tries not to be biased.

A floral designer for eighteen years, **Janet Frye** owns the Enchanted Florist in Arden, North Carolina, and Tootsie, a smiling Gemini cocker-keeshond.

Liz Fye, of Seattle, is co-owner and operator of Flytes of Fancy, which makes outfits for cats and dogs, a business she's in because of her oldest pomeranian, Coco. A member of Seattle Purebred Dog Rescue, Liz presently shares her home with three other pomeranians and her husband.

Mike Hester owns and operates Hester's Lothlorien, a custom woodworking business featuring native hardwoods in Asheville, North Carolina; he grew up with dogs but fell from grace and turned into a cat person.

Daisy Mae, a border collie-beagle mix, adopted **Diane** and **Rolf Holmquist**, of Micaville, North Carolina. Diane's creative passions are traditional quilts and children's clothes.

Rolf Holmquist, printmaker and artist extraordinaire, has lately been turning found wood into bat houses and is building a cabin in the woods near Burnsville, North Carolina.

Dana Irwin, a painter and graphic designer, is the art director who designed this book and shares her home with Parker, a border collie.

An unabashed cat person, **Suzanne Koppi** is a long-time special education teacher who sews for relaxation in Black Mountain, North Caroina.

A former member of the Dog Gift of the Month Club and former owner of a soft-coated Wheaton terrier, Sprite, and a Kerry-blue terrier,

Garth, **Nancy McGaha** creates original beadwork and needlework in Swannanoa, North Carolina.

Debbie Midkiff owns the Weed Patch in Barboursville, West Virginia, where she dispenses natural pet-care products (she signs her correspondence "herbally yours").

Genna Miles, of Manteo, North Carolina, spins dog and cat hair into custom hats and teaches spinning at workshops and in the public schools.

Dolly Lutz Morris turns her hand to many crafts, is the author of *The Flower Drying Handbook* (Sterling, 1996), and even though she has eight cats is sympathetic to dogs and dog people.

Award-winning poet and fiction writer **Enid Shomer** for years bred Irish water spaniels, is a longtime crocheter and knitter, and has recently turned her life over to Sonnet, a papillon; they share a pad in New York City.

An avid cross-stitcher for fifteen years, **Garnette Sprinkle** is a lifetime Madison County, North Carolina, resident and a retired public-health nurse.

Wood sculptor **Mark Strom** recently finished sculpting a life-sized Saint Francis and lives in a zoo—two dogs, five cats, a cockatiel, and three kids.

Terry Taylor, a former kindergarten teacher, is an out-of-control craftsperson who turns his talented hand to a remarkable variety of crafts.

Suzann Thompson, who recently moved to Sheffield, England, with three dogs (and her husband and infant daughter), designs for Monsanto's Designs for America Program.

Kim Tibbals-Thompson, whose father raised hunting dogs, is an art director and graphic designer who expends lots of artistic energy in drawing, sewing, herbal crafts, gardening, and broom making in Asheville, North Carolina.

Cheryl Weiderspahn lives on a dairy farm near Cochranton, Pennsylvania, with a collie-St. Bernard mix, Miriam, and owns a pattern company, Homestead Specialties.

Although **Pamella (Wil) Wilson**, an accomplished potter and visual artist, can't have a dog in her Asheville, North Carolina, apartment, her house-sitting business gives her a big family of dogs (and cats).

Maryn Wynne of Lakeville, Minnesota, co-owns and operates Flytes of Fancy, a feline and canine clothing accessory business.

Contributing Dogs

A short-haired Jack Russell terrier whose best friend is a fat tabby named Bing, BOBBIE is three but in his heart will be forever a two-year-old, according to his other best friend, Lisa Ohler.

A highly friendly Chihuahua mix, year-old CHAMP hangs out at Broadway Video in Asheville with the store's new owner, Chris Yountz; both are North Carolinians.

All five four-legged Fraziers were rescued from neglectful homes as adults and have traveled in a motor home from the Arctic Circle to Key West with Nancy and John Wayne Frazier. BOOTS is a forty-pound black mix; PITA, an eighteen-pound rat terrier; and ANGEL, "T," and TIPPY are toy fox terriers; all are well behaved, obedient, and endearing..

Emily and Rachel's CELIE GIRL—Celie for short, named after The Color Purple heroine—is a miniature Doberman pinscher born in May 1992. She sleeps with her head on Vicky Lacy's pillow and sits in window sills and purrs, trying to be a cat.

Born in Oxford, North Carolina, one-year-old EMMA has grown from a feisty puppy into a friendly Labrador retriever with a heavy social schedule; she loves to travel, her ears blowing in the wind, with Laura Dover and Patrick Doran.

Shar-pei chums EMMETT and SUMMONER live with Ashely Siegel (the wrinkle-free one); by a happy coincidence, both dogs were born July 12, 1993, Emmett in Tryon, North Carolina, and Summoner in Beaverton, Oregon.

The lovely **HAVANA**, a seventy-pound weimaraner born in April 1995 in Lexington, North Carolina, can run forever alongside Matt Ragaller's bike; her other favorite activity (it's her sporting-dog genes) is carrying things around in her mouth.

Five of the eight-puppy first litter of golden retrievers **LEONARD OF HAMBURG** and **DIXIE'S AMBER WAVE** posed like pros at age two months, at home at Dixie Barkdoll's in Weaverville, North Carolina.

IVORY, a gentle cocker spaniel, has lived with Gary Jamison since he witnessed her birth fourteen years ago in Sylva, North Carolina. At 8:45 every night, she barks to remind him it's nearly nine o'clock and time for her bedtime snack bones.

KOSMO (named for Seinfeld's maniacal Kramer), an eight-month-old Jack Russell terrier and North Carolina native, has already been to obedience school with Susan Anderson, whom he keeps entertained—and busy.

The happy and award-winning golden retriever family of **NICK**, **BRANDY**, **TEDDY**, and **BUDDY** are the beautifully behaved companions of agility, conformation, and obedience trainer Jean Bjork McAloon and Tim McAloon of Weaverville, North Carolina. Their diminutive pal, **HOLLY**, is a Cavalier King Charles.

A rare olde English bulldogge, **JACK** is a Massachusetts native, three years old, and sixty-five pounds of muscle, obedience, and personality, who brings joy and laughter into the life of Erin Tallon of Marshall, North Carolina.

Florida-born **JADE**, a four-year-old German shepherd mix, was adopted from the shelter in Key West, where she loved retrieving coconuts from the Gulf of Mexico; she is the best friend of Holly Decker.

123

ROMEO, *an independent-minded seven-year-old spitz, was socially promoted in obedience training after flunking three times and, now that he lives in the community of Grapevine, North Carolina, with Jennifer Cason, no longer needs tranquilizers. Four-year-old* SAMANTHA, *a Chesapeake Bay retriever-lab-greyhound mix, aptly hails from Back Bay, Virginia, and now belongs to Dennis Cason.*

PARKER, *a two-year-old border collie who lives with Dana Irwin, the designer and art director for this book, is a bright, lovable foundling who can open doors and herds anything that moves, including Dana's cats.*

Adopted from the local shelter, ROMMIE *(for Rommel) is a Jack Russell mix, one and a half, who pals around with an older female,* DIXIE, *a cocker mix named for the Winn-Dixie where she was rescued going through the trash. Both now live with Kendall McDevitt in Weaverville, North Carolina.*

The dapper and peace-loving bull terrier SPARTA, *eight years old and fifty pounds, lives in Burnsville, North Carolina, with Gil and Joyce Johnson, where for fun he rams heads with his best friend, Winston, an English bulldog.*

Named for one of the 101 dalmatians, PENNY *arrived boxed and wrapped under Terry and Lauren Northup's Christmas tree in 1991. She's a mountain hiker, a squirrel stalker, and a one-way retriever (she fetches but doesn't come back).*

A Manhattan resident, SONNET, a papillon, is a certified service dog as well as a top-flight model; she picks up pens, knitting needles, and car keys for her friend, poet Enid Shomer, who in return knits her wardrobe and sings her praises.

An Arizona native, five-year-old TAIWANEY is 85 percent wolf, 15 percent husky who has adapted well to the North Carolina mountains, where she lives with Rosemary Kast.

A Maltese from Minnesota, weighing in at six pounds, two-year-old WILLIE gets his silky hair brushed every morning by Nita De Salme in Weaverville, North Carolina.

SOPHIE, an old English sheepdog, and BOCCA, a dachsund, chose to migrate with their pal Jan Cope from Florida to Asheville, North Carolina, where they say they're glad it's cooler but the dogs don't talk right.

Adopted from an animal shelter, WATSON, a one-year-old Australian shepherd mix, is a cat herder whose hobby is chewing, both activities he practices at home with D. V. Talbert in Asheville, North Carolina.

WINSTON of Asheville, a six-month-old English springer spaniel, appropriately lives with Lisa and Rice Yorty at the Lion and the Rose, an English-style bed and breakfast in Asheville, North Carolina; descended from a long line of champions, Winston was especially bred to be a pacifist.

YANKEE (but born in Augusta, Georgia), a well-traveled Boston terrier of one and a half years, can't get out of the South—now he lives and models in Asheville, North Carolina, with Carol Renton.

125

Acknowledgments

Thanks...

to Jasmine Bianca McAdams, who modeled the Puppy Love Toddler Sweat Suit and posed with the Welcome-Home Puppy Cushion; she's three and loves to sing, dress up, and paint her nails...to Lisa Yorty, incredibly hospitable owner and host of Asheville, North Carolina's The Lion and the Rose bed and breakfast, who opened the inn and its lovely grounds for hours of photography shoots (pages 22-23, 27, 29, 33, 69, 95, 96)...for the loan of props (all in Asheville): Super Petz (pages 20, 69, 72, 85, 92, 93); Lexington Park Antiques (pages 36, 37); The Natural Home (page 79); Shirley Turner, of Cross Stitch Corner (page 98); and Chief John Rukavina and Connie Jones of the Asheville Fire Department (page 75)...for their charming garden, Clyde Savings Bank of Asheville... for dog-finding help, Katherine Cartilege of Asheville's Groomers on the Go and Jan Cope... for the photos on page 41, Regina Neumeister and Kathy Foreman, NEADS... and especially to all the dogs and their companions, who let us take far more pictures than a sensible dog should have to stand for.